HOW TO
PUBLISH
^A BOOK

Novels by Nathan Bransford:

Jacob Wonderbar and the Cosmic Space Kapow
Jacob Wonderbar for President of the Universe
Jacob Wonderbar and the Interstellar Time Warp

Books on writing and publishing
by Nathan Bransford:

How to Write a Novel
How to Publish a Book

HOW TO
PUBLISH
A BOOK

41 RULES FOR SUCCESSFULLY PUBLISHING
A BOOK THAT YOU WILL LOVE FOREVER

NATHAN
BRANSFORD

PREPARATION

Rule #1
IT ALL STARTS WITH A GREAT BOOK

Chances are, if you are reading this book, you have finished writing a book or at the very least have a killer idea for one.

This is amazing! Well done.

And now you might be thinking ... Um, what do I do with this magical creation I have brought forth into the world?

In this guide, you will find everything you need to see your book through to successful publication, whether this is via traditional publishing with one of the "Big Five" publishers (Penguin Random House, HarperCollins, Simon & Schuster, Macmillan,

Hachette), a smaller independent publisher (like Tin House, Soho Press, or Beacon Press), self-publishing (like Amazon Kindle Direct Publishing and IngramSpark), or hybrid publishing (like Greenleaf and Mascot Books). Or trying traditional publishing first and then self-publishing later, or self-publishing, selling a bazillion copies, and then entertaining offers from traditional publishers from the comfort of your yacht. Anything is possible!

You too can have your book out in the wild.

Take it from me: I've seen the publishing world from every angle. I used to be a literary agent, where I represented writers and helped shepherd their books to successful publication with major publishers. Then I went and wrote a trilogy that was published by Penguin. Then I self-published a guide to writing a novel, as well as the very guide you are now holding in your hands.

What all these experiences taught me is that although every path to publication is different, there are some relatively straightforward steps you can follow to increase your odds of finding the smoothest, happiest possible path to successful publication. The publishing process may seem opaque and mysterious from the outside, but I'm here to break it all down for you.

This book's content admittedly skews a bit toward traditional publication because 1) there are more customs to abide by in traditional publishing, whereas there's more freedom in self-publishing, and 2) self-publishing is changing so rapidly that I'm mainly sticking to tried-and-true principles that should carry you through even as the platforms evolve. But, within these pages you should find everything you need to understand both processes. (And if you don't find everything you need: tell me! I'll fix it.)

First, though, some real talk.

You're probably not going to get rich because of your book. You might! But probably not.

Your book is not going to solve all of your problems.

Your book is not going to cure cancer, stop the Earth from rotating on its axis, or give the Cowardly Lion his courage. (Only the Wizard of Oz can do that ... duh.)

Discouraged? Don't be.

You really can do this!

You just need to be in this for the right reasons. Or should I say, reason. There is only one: **you love your book and want it to find readers who will love it, too.**

It's impossible to predict a book's success in advance, and your book is going to find the audience it's going to find. It may be ten readers, it may be a hundred million readers, or it may one day be beamed into space and become a wild bestseller on Planet Zog.

Do you know how you can tell how many copies you will sell in advance?

(No, really, do you? Because if you do, please email me so that we can go into business together: nathan@nathanbransford.com)

Chances are you will not be able to predict your success. Instead, it will be left to your marketing skills and the whims of fate. And this is totally fine!

Most importantly, whatever happens, however many copies you sell, whatever terrible reviews you get on Planet Zog, your book will be something that you will be proud of for the rest of your life. No one will ever be able to take away the fact that you wrote a book and published it. It's an incredible journey to wind up with a book in your hands.

Let me repeat. YOUR book. IN YOUR HANDS. It's a magical feeling.

But how *do* you get the darn thing published?

Read on, my friend.

Rule #2
UNDERSTAND HOW THE TRADITIONAL PUBLISHING PROCESS WORKS

Before you make any decisions about the best path for your book, it's first advisable to take a moment, learn about how this whole shebang works, and then decide how best to proceed with all the facts at your disposal.

Let's start by reviewing the traditional publishing process. (We'll get to a similar overview of self-publishing and hybrid publishing in Rule #3.)

So here goes: the basics of how a book gets published through your Penguin Random Houses and your Simon & Schusters. Most of the books you see in bookstores were birthed by the process outlined in this chapter.

For a first-time author, a book generally starts with a completely finished and polished manuscript for fiction (and memoirs by non-celebrities) and with a book proposal and sample pages for nonfiction (I cover proposals in Rule #10).

Yes, novelists: you have to write the whole thing. Once you establish yourself as a writer, one or two published books down the line, it may be possible to sell a novel on a partial—100 or so pages of the book in progress—but it's still pretty rare.

So your first step is to complete and perfect your work. This means seeking editing and feedback, which are imperative. You should not be relying on a mere good idea to carry you through to publication. Your manuscript or proposal needs to be as polished as you can possibly make it *before* anything else, and even then you will likely have further editing to do as you make your way along this journey.

I can't emphasize this enough: you *must* polish your work before you embark on the traditional publishing process. This means getting feedback from editors you trust, going through multiple rounds of revisions, and doing everything you can to make your book as strong as possible before you even start down this road. (Note: reach out to me if you would

like professional help editing your work: nathan@
nathanbransford.com)

Once your manuscript or nonfiction book proposal
shines like the top of the Chrysler Building, you may
proceed to the next step.

GET A LITERARY AGENT

One of the keys to the traditional publishing path
is finding a literary agent. Very few publishers accept
submissions from un-agented authors, so this is a
nearly essential step to be published by one of the Big
5 publishers or one of their imprints. Smaller publishers are not as strict about receiving un-agented
submissions, but even with small presses having an
agent is usually in your best interest.

Your agent is the person who will represent your
work and share it with editors at different publishing
houses with whom the agent has relationships and
believes will be the best champion. A good agent can
give a project a better chance at succeeding and will
usually be able to negotiate a better deal than you
would be able to achieve on your own. An agent will
then shepherd you through the publishing process
and be an advocate and advisor for your writing
career in general. (For a complete overview of what
agents do, see Rule #7.)

If the book sells, the agent gets 15% of the proceeds
from the book for domestic sales and 20% for foreign

sales. Alternatively, if the book doesn't sell to a publisher, the agent gets a big old fancy pile of nothing. (Other than recouping incidental fees, like photocopying and postage.) So, trust me, an agent wants your book to sell. And they wouldn't have agreed to represent the project if they didn't have good-faith confidence that it would sell.

We will talk more in depth about how to find an agent later on, but for now, know that you will almost assuredly need one in order to find a publisher.

THE SUBMISSION PROCESS

Once an agent has taken on a project, they may work with you on some revisions to make the manuscript/proposal as strong as possible before submission. When it's ready, the agent will break out the old rolodex they've built through years of networking and send the submission to the editors at various publishers who they feel are most appropriate for the book.

The agent will then "submit" your book to a select group of editors for consideration, usually 5–10 initially, followed by additional rounds as needed, but occasionally an agent will send to one editor in particular as an "exclusive" if they think there's a perfect fit.

Bear in mind, this submission process—the time it takes various editors to read your book and decide if it's the right fit for them or not—can take anywhere

9

from a week to a year or more depending on how long it takes the agent to find a match for the project. You may also be asked to meet with an editor in person or have a phone conversation as a part of this process.

If an editor receives a submission they're interested in acquiring, they will share it with their colleagues and boss(es) to gauge their enthusiasm. Once the editor has the go-ahead to move forward with the project, they will send the agent an offer. Huzzah! An offer!

Editors have many roles beyond acquiring books and editing them. In fact, editing is really just a sliver of their full responsibilities. An editor functions more like a product manager for a book, coordinating all the different tasks that need to be completed in order to publish, everything from acquisitions to writing jacket copy to developing marketing materials to drumming up enthusiasm for the book among their sales teams. Their job is to make sure everyone is excited about your book and that it will find an audience.

All to say, a good editor is your partner in creating the very best version of your work and will serve as a steadfast cheerleader for it.

NEGOTIATION

The central points of consideration for an offer usually constitute the advance, royalties, and the countries/territories the publisher can sell into, and then there are a range of other specific terms that your publisher and agent will work through.

There's more detailed information on publishing contracts in Rule #22 and a glossary with publishing terminology in Rule #40, but here are the two most important terms.

The **advance** is a payment from the publisher to the author, usually divided into installments, which the author keeps regardless of how many copies the book sells. (Assuming the author fulfills all the terms of the agreement.)

The **royalties** are a percentage of every copy sold. Proceeds from the royalties first go toward paying down the advance that the publisher paid the author. (But again, the author doesn't have to pay back the advance if they don't sell enough copies.) After the advance is covered by the royalties, which is called "earning out," the royalties then go to the author.

Here's an example. If an author receives a $50,000 advance with hardcover royalties of 10% of the list price on a book that's listed for sale at $25, they need to sell 20,000 copies to earn out. How that breaks down: $2.50 per copy (10% of the list price) x 20,000 copies sold = $50,000 advance. Afterward, the author will receive $2.50 for every additional copy sold. The agent will receive 15% of the $50,000 advance as well as 15% of the royalties (if the book earns out).

Sometimes the offer from the publisher will be for

one book or sometimes it will be for multiple books. If more than one editor is interested in the project, an agent may ask all the editors for their best offers or the agent may hold an auction to determine which publisher will bid the highest.

When the deal points have been agreed upon and you accept an offer, the publisher will send a contract, which the agent or the agency's contracts director will negotiate all the way down to the fine print. Some of these deal points get into the nitty gritty, so it helps to trust and empower your agent in this process to review and negotiate with your best interests in mind.

Also, bear in mind that if you try to work with a publisher directly, you should consult with an attorney who specializes in book publishing deals, rather than one who is just familiar with contracts generally, because there are particular customs unique to the publishing industry that are important to know.

THE PATH TO PUBLICATION

After the contract has been signed, if the project was sold on proposal, it's time for you to write the book. The contract will specify the delivery dates, which are negotiated in advance.

Once the manuscript is completed (nonfiction) or after the contract is signed (fiction), the editor will usually send an editorial letter suggesting content changes. (Despite popular belief, editors *do* still edit.)

These revisions are somewhat negotiable, but for the most part you'd be wise to follow your editor's suggestions or, at the very least, have an open mind.

When the changes have been made and the manuscript is deemed editorially acceptable, it moves to copyediting, where typos and other errors are corrected, and the text is laid out and designed for how it will look on the pages of the final book.

It is your responsibility as the author to also carefully review the manuscript in the various production stages to catch errors or typos. The publisher is working during this time on the design of the book, including the cover, trim size, paper type, and other designy considerations. Believe it or not, authors don't typically have approval over their cover, but they may be consulted.

Meanwhile, the editor is coordinating with their marketing and sales teams, writing the jacket copy, hopefully generating enthusiasm within the publisher for the project, and helping to shape marketing plans. Several months before the book's publication, the sales team will be coordinating with bookstore buyers and other "accounts" as they place their orders, which helps determine how many copies of the book the publisher prints.

The sales force's communication with national chains and independent booksellers is a very important step because it's key to a publisher's distribution.

One of the main differences between traditional and self-publishing is that publishers have distribution channels that get books into bookstores, airports, supermarkets, and wherever else print books are sold.

All along the way, the agent keeps tabs with the publisher throughout to make sure everything is happening according to plan.

The publication process, from finished manuscript to books on sale, usually takes a year or more. It can occasionally be compressed if the book is an especially timely project, but the various steps described above typically require quite a bit of lead time.

PUBLICATION!

When the publication date arrives, the book goes on sale and you, promising author, become rich and famous beyond your wildest dreams. Sometimes. Not usually.

In reality, you will need to do everything within your power to help market the book, whether that's a social media blitz, bookstore appearances, or television and radio appearances. (More on marketing in Rule #36.)

You then get cracking on your next book and the process repeats.

There you have it!

UNDERSTAND HOW SELF-PUBLISHING AND HYBRID PUBLISHING WORK

Now for self-publishing and hybrid publishing.

First up: self-publishing. The best way to wrap your head around the self-publishing process is to break it down into the eight essential steps that go into creating the book, whether that's a print edition, e-book, or both. You can do these steps yourself, you can farm them out to people who will happily take your money to do them for you, or you can do a mix, but you must do these eight things in order to have a quality book.

One important thing to remember about self-publishing is that you do not have agents and other publishing employees who are guiding you through this process and handling them for you. You need to figure it out yourself, which requires a certain level of entrepreneurialism.

I'll go into all of these steps in greater depth later in the book, but for now, here's a basic overview of the steps that go into self-publishing a book:

#1. WRITE THE DARN THING

When self-publishing, first, you write the book. All the way, whether it's fiction or nonfiction. (Or you'll need to pay a ghostwriter.)

Not done yet? Oh sorry, I'll wait.

...

How about now? Okay, cool.

#2. EDIT IT

There are two main stages of editing, and they're separate and distinct: **developmental editing** and **copyediting**.

A developmental edit is where someone reads your book to suggest improvements in structure, plot, pacing, character development, dialogue, etc.

These edits can come from a paid editor, a critique partner, a friend, a spouse, someone who lives in a van down by the river ... whoever they are, they should help you get your manuscript into better shape than you could achieve on your own. You should get help from both an overall structural and plot perspective and on a more granular level, with line edits to smooth and refine the prose. (More on this in Rule #28.)

Once you have finished making all the improvements that you and your editor(s) can possibly think to make, you then need a copyeditor who will spot typeoes, grammar problem and inconsistent uses of Oxford commas. These copyediting creatures are wondrous, eagle-eyed beings, heaven sent for those of us who wouldn't be able to spot a typo if it punched us in the face.

Now you have yourself a finished and polished manuscript.

#3. FIGURE OUT HOW AND WHERE YOU WANT TO PUBLISH

There are two main formats to consider when self-publishing: paperback and e-books.

There are ways to produce hardcover books if you really want to, but as of this writing the economics of self-publishing are primarily oriented toward e-books and print-on-demand paperback books. The advantage of print on demand is that you don't have to pay any up-front costs to print a book. They will print the copies only when customers buy them.

With e-books, you can choose to make your book available exclusively via Amazon's Kindle platform, which is by far the most popular format, or you can go nonexclusive and also make it available via the smaller e-booksellers.

Decide where you want to publish your books early because it will impact which materials you will need before you publish.

#4. WRITE YOUR COVER COPY AND MARKETING MATERIALS

Wait. Write marketing materials already?

Yep.

Authors are notorious for bristling at being forced to distill the beauty of their long and beautifully complicated works into succinct descriptions.

You have to do it. And do it as early as possible because you'll need marketing copy before you design your cover.

(We'll cover more about how to write good pitches in Rule #5.)

#5. DESIGN YOUR INTERIOR

I bet you didn't think about this step, did you? When you open up a professionally designed book, do you notice how wonderfully aligned everything is? Do you notice how the different fonts are complementary? Do you notice how the margins feel pleasing to the eye even though they account for the seam in the middle of the book?

Well. You may *not* have noticed, but that's the point. It's just pleasing in a way you can take for granted.

This doesn't happen by accident. You'll need to make sure everything on the inside has a clean, visually pleasing layout that also accounts for the various quirks in different e-book formats.

#6. DESIGN THE COVER

Woo! Woooooo!!

This is the fun part. You probably even sketched out fifty versions of your cover while you were procrastinating. I know I did, and my drawing ability is so bad it looks like I held the pen with my feet. Didn't care.

Unlike traditional publishing, where your publisher will often simply show you your cover and ask you how much you like it on a scale of "love it" to "simply stunning," one of the best things about self-publishing is that you have total control over your cover. Heck, you could even swap out the covers on your books once a week if you wanted to.

Your work here may be as simple as designing a single rectangular image, if you're going e-book only, or a full-fledged cover with a front, back, and spine if you're going for print. That's why it's helpful to know in advance which route you're going to pursue. Check the different publishers for their requirements to be sure you have the right-sized covers.

#7. FIGURE OUT YOUR PRICE POINT AND GET EVERYTHING UPLOADED

Once you have all the files you need from your interior designer and cover designer, all that's left is getting everything uploaded and published.

When I self-published my first book, I found the process of uploading the book way easier than I thought it would be.

Technology is a wondrous thing!

#8. MARKET THE HECK OUT OF IT

Unless you already have an established platform, the most challenging element of self-publishing is the last one: marketing your book.

The key thing to know about marketing is that there are millions of ways to go about it, so you'll need to pick and choose your approach. But, you're going to have to do *something* if you want people to find your book and read it.

(For more on marketing, see Rule #36.)

And that's it! Once you've accomplished these eight steps, you'll have yourself a self-published book that you can flog to everyone you know.

HYBRID PUBLISHING

Now for hybrid publishing.

Hybrid publishing isn't quite traditional publishing and isn't quite self-publishing. Essentially, a hybrid publisher takes on some or all the functions of a traditional publisher, such as editing, design, and distribution, but authors shoulder more of the initial investment than with traditional publishing in the form of initial fees. Hybrid publishers typically offer royalties that are higher than traditional publishing but lower than self-publishing.

In theory, hybrid publishers provide you value by offering better design, production, and print distribution than you would be able to achieve on your own via self-publishing, but you earn less on a per-copy basis than if you managed the self-publishing process yourself. Some hybrid publishers are selective in the authors they choose to take on, others are more like assisted-publishing models that will take on all comers.

Some authors appreciate having the publishing process managed for them and are willing to pay a premium to avoid getting caught in the self-publishing weeds. Or you might come across a hybrid publisher who genuinely adds value through their design or distribution. At worst, a hybrid publisher is really just a scam artist in disguise, taking advantage of the buzz around hybrid publishing and exploiting your ego to charge you top dollar for things you don't need.

It's tough to generalize about hybrid publishing because there are so many different models with so many differing levels of legitimacy, and it's a land-scape that's changing quickly.

No matter which path you pursue (and there's more on how to choose in Rule #6), make sure you proceed only after some thorough research.

Rule #4
PROPERLY FORMAT YOUR MANUSCRIPT

A whole rule for formatting? Really?

Trust me. It matters. As a former literary agent and current author coach, let me tell you that it's shocking how few aspiring authors follow industry standard formatting.

And yes, this rule applies even if you're pursuing self-publishing. Chances are you'll be engaging at some point with freelancers with professional publishing experience who are used to working with manuscripts that adhere to this format, and even if you're not, starting with this format will save you from spending hours cleaning up wonky formatting as you produce your interior design.

I've seen a whole lot of manuscripts in my day, and sometimes it feels like no two manuscripts have ever been formatted the same way. This means I have seen everything from single-spaced 10-point font with half-inch margins to double-spaced 24-point font.

So how should you format your manuscript? Here's the industry standard template. Know it. Use it. Live it.

- Double spaced
- 1-inch margins
- Half-inch indent for a new paragraph (use the automatic indent function in your word processing program or use tabs. Don't use spaces)
- Numbered pages (and make sure the page numbers don't start over every chapter)
- Page break at the end of a chapter (use the page break function in your word processing program)
- A default 12-point font, preferably Times New Roman. No matter how much Gill Sans Ultra Bold Condensed is calling your name, and believe me I know how tempting you can be, Gill Sans Ultra Bold Condensed, you wily devil you ... just resist.
- No fiddling at all with anything else. No messing with the spacing before and after paragraphs, no fiddling with the width of the type, no full justification, no hyphenation. Basically, just open up Word or Pages, hit double spacing, make

HOW TO PUBLISH A BOOK

sure the pages are numbered, set up half-inch indents, and start typing.

- And most importantly: **don't try to make it look like the layout of a book.**

If you want to get more granular, for chapter titles I hit the return button twice, center the chapter title, hit return twice again, and then start with the first paragraph. This gives a bit of a visual break without needlessly padding my page count with a ton of space at the top. Also: one space after periods.

If you're submitting to literary agents, it can also be helpful to create a title page with your contact information and include your last name in the header along with the page numbers, in case the literary agent prints out a bunch of manuscripts and then gets caught in a wind storm.

Following the industry standard format is one of the absolute easiest things you can do to look like you know what you're doing.

So do it!

Rule #5
HONE YOUR PITCH

One thing that writers tend to hate is summarizing their work. Loathe! Abhor! Hiss!

Yes, we're getting the sticky things out of the way first.

Some authors feel it is simply beneath their dignity to have to distill the wondrous complexity of their book into a brief summation.

Here's the problem. Summarizing your work is simply part of the job description of being an author. You signed up for it the minute you typed "Chapter 1." (And yes, literary fiction types, you don't get to sail through on "Oh man, it's so complicated but it's really all about the writing." You have to pitch, too!) Whether it's pitching a project to an editor, for film, in interviews, or in everyday conversation, you'll basically spend about as much time summarizing and talking about your work as you did writing it.

If you're trying to find a literary agent, you'll probably need to write a query letter. If you're self-publishing, you'll need to write good jacket copy (or at least know what good jacket copy looks like). When you're telling acquaintances what your book is about, you'll need to avoid making them fall asleep.

You get the idea.

Start thinking about your pitch early and then you can spend time honing it.

THE ONE-SENTENCE PITCH

The one-sentence pitch is at the heart of all of your other pitches. It's the essence of your book, the line you'll dash off when you just want to briefly tell people about your book but still make it sound awesome.

A one-sentence pitch is by no means easy to write. You need to do it anyway.

There are three basic elements in a good one-sentence pitch for a novel or memoir. (We'll get to nonfiction in a sec.)

- The conflict that sets the protagonist on their journey
- The obstacle
- The quest

The quest can be a physical or interior journey, but it's what happens to the character(s) between the beginning of the plot and the end. The opening conflict is the first step in this quest. It's how the journey begins. The obstacle is what stands in the way of this journey.

Hopefully you'll also add some unique details that give the flavor of your novel.

The resulting very basic pitch is like this: When OPENING CONFLICT happens to CHARACTER(s), they have OVERCOME CONFLICT to COMPLETE QUEST.

There are lots different ways of structuring these basic elements, but they should be there.

For instance, for my novel *Jacob Wonderbar and the Cosmic Space Kapow*, this was my one-sentence pitch:

Three kids trade a corndog (FLAVOR) for a spaceship, blast off into space (OPENING CONFLICT), accidentally break the universe (OBSTACLE), and have to find their way back home (QUEST).

If I were writing a one-sentence pitch for *Eat Pray Love*, it would be as follows:

A recently divorced woman (OPENING CONFLICT) travels (QUEST) to Italy for pleasure,

India for spirituality, and Bali for balance (INNER OBSTACLES), but she finds love instead (FLAVOR).

Even if you're writing self-help or prescriptive nonfiction, this structure isn't a bad one to emulate. Rather than a character's journey, you'll want to get at the nubby essence of your book. It's the selling point, the promise that the book is going to fulfill.

Some of the all-time best one-sentence pitches for nonfiction, in my opinion, are the actual book titles *He's Just Not That Into You* and *The Life-Changing Magic of Tidying Up,* which convey the essence of the books in a clear and powerful way.

ONE PARAGRAPH AND TWO PARAGRAPH PITCHES

While a good one-sentence pitch will carry you through most situations where you just need to dash off what your book is about, it can be helpful to have one and two paragraph pitches to draw upon when the situation calls for more detail, such as query letters and jacket copy.

With one-paragraph and two-paragraph pitches, you have a bit more latitude to add detail to illustrate more about your plot and the world of your novel or, in the case of nonfiction, the scope of your project.

In order to do this, a good place to start is with the middle section of my patent-pending (not really)

Query Letter Template, which we'll cover more in depth in Rule #13:

- [protagonist name] is a [description of protagonist] living in [setting]. But when [complicating incident], [protagonist name] must [protagonist's quest] and [verb] [villain] in order to [protagonist's goal].

This will give you a basic description that you will likely need to expand upon. But in one-paragraph and two-paragraph pitches, it's helpful to make sure that all of these elements are present.

To show you how I did it, here are my one-paragraph and two-paragraph pitches for *Jacob Wonderbar*:

ONE PARAGRAPH:

Jacob Wonderbar trades a corndog for a sassy spaceship and blasts off into space with his best friends, Sarah and Dexter. After they accidentally break the universe in a giant space kapow, a nefarious space pirate named Mick Cracken maroons Jacob and Dexter on a tiny planet that smells like burp breath. They have to work together to make it back to their street on Earth where all the houses look the same.

TWO PARAGRAPH:

Jacob Wonderbar has been the bane of every substitute teacher at Magellan Middle School ever since his dad moved away from home. He never would have survived without his best friend Dexter, even if he is a little timid, and his cute-but-tough friend Sarah Daisy, who is chronically overscheduled.

But when the trio meets a mysterious man in silver they trade a corn dog for his sassy spaceship and blast off into the great unknown. That is, until they break the universe in a giant space kapow and a nefarious space buccaneer named Mick Cracken maroons Jacob and Dexter on a tiny planet that smells like burp breath. The friends have to work together to make it back to their little street where the houses look the same, even as Earth seems farther and farther away.

As you're fleshing out your pitch, I find that it's far more successful to try as much as possible to stick to what literally happens in your book. Stay away from themes or the lessons your characters learn, which can sound trite and generic, and instead show us what happens in your novel with key details that bring your particular setting and characters to life.

For nonfiction, consider adding a bit more about your qualifications and try to weave in the key selling points for your project. Imagine you're in a bookstore with someone holding a copy of your book in their hand and you need to tell them why they should buy it. You want to include a bit more about the key promise of your book, plus why you're the best person to have written it.

KNOW YOUR GENRE

As you're crafting your pitch, it's also helpful to know your genre or category so that you can take this into account in how you position your novel. (Genres are the specific flavor of book you're writing, like romantic suspense or New Age, while categories are more general, like bookstore shelves: think General/ Adult Fiction or Self-Help).

Much like summaries, authors often bristle at having to choose one genre. It seems like an unfair constraint cooked up in some foreboding tower by a cackling publisher, who maniacally decreed one day that authors everywhere must sort themselves into categories before being allowed to enter the gates.

But it's very important to know where either a novel or a nonfiction book will sit on the shelf (or virtual shelf), and it's helpful to figure this out relatively early in both the traditional and self-publishing process so you can factor it into your pitches.

If you plan to pursue traditional publishing, you'll need to know your genre at least in part because literary agents and publishers tend to specialize in particular genres. When you are researching literary agents, knowing your genre will help narrow down the agents who might be a fit for you. As you move through the publishing process, agents will then target editors at particular publishing houses, who in turn have sales and marketing teams that are all oriented around knowing their area of specialty. These tend to be highly calibrated to particular genres.

But it's not just agents and publishers who care about genre. Who else cares?

Readers.

Walk into a bookstore. You'll see that sections are arranged by categories. Go to Amazon or BN.com. The sections are arranged by categories, and you can also drill down into particular genres.

These sections don't exist as a means to torture authors. They exist because readers often know what they are looking for ahead of time and are browsing for something in particular and will head straight to that section. This is why knowing your genre is helpful if you're self-publishing, too, although one of the benefits of self-publishing is that you have a bit more freedom in this regard.

It's not romantic to be forced to shoehorn your book into summaries and genres, but a bit of thought and preparation will help save you from a great deal of heartache down the line.

Rule #6
CHART YOUR COURSE

To self-publish or traditionally publish or hybrid publish. That is the question.

Whether tis nobler in the mind to suffer the slings and arrows of agents and publishers or to take arms against a sea of books on Amazon, and by being among them, rise above? To die, to sleep (oh wait, you won't), to sleep perchance to dream of fame and riches ... aye there's the rub.

Ahem. Sorry.

Translation: Should you try your luck with agents and publishers? Should you just go ahead and self-publish and see how it sells? Should you try agents and publishers first and then self-publish if that doesn't work? What about that whole hybrid thing?

Here are eight questions to ask yourself to help you decide:

1] IS YOUR BOOK A NICHE/PASSION PROJECT OR DOES IT HAVE BROAD, NATIONAL APPEAL?

In order to attract a traditional publisher, especially one of the major ones, you're going to need to have a book that fits squarely into an established genre and has mass commercial appeal.

Be honest with yourself. Is your book something that has the potential to be read by a broad audience or does it appeal to a smaller niche? Is it a potential bestseller or something you just wrote to, say, have your family history recorded for posterity?

Let's say you are thinking about writing a book of nonfiction and want to have it published by a major publisher. The first thing you need to do is assume that every single person in the entire world wants to write a book (which isn't really an assumption, as it's basically true).

The second thing you need to do is ask yourself if you are one of the most qualified people in the entire world to write and promote this book. This applies to virtually all nonfiction.

If you want to write a cookbook, are you a nationally recognized chef or on the Food Network? If you want to write about terrorism, are you one of the world's foremost experts on terrorism? If you want to write about an historical event or period, are you a decorated journalist or historian?

Heck, if you want to write a book about extraterrestrial encounters, are you an internationally recognized expert on extraterrestrial encounters?

If the answer to that question is no, then sorry, chances are you're not going to get your book published by a major publisher. If you can imagine someone out there who is more qualified than you to write a book, then that person probably already has his or her proposal in front of publishers as we speak.

In the publishing industry, this is called "platform," which is a combination of your authority as an author and the audience you can draw upon to promote your book, such as a blog, social media following, or access to major media. Publishers want to know that you are one of—if not THE— best people in the entire world to be writing and promoting this book. Platform is essential for nonfiction, and having an existing audience is helpful (but not mandatory) for fiction.

If your book is hyper-specialized, such as a regional travel guide or oriented toward the academic market, you might want to either try for a similarly specialized/academic publisher or just go ahead and self-publish. If it's a passion project without commercial potential, you're probably best-served going straight to self-publishing.

2] DO YOU HAVE A REASONABLE WORD COUNT?

I'm going to share an uncomfortable truth for all the prodigiously verbose or taciturn writers among us: **word count matters.**

Writing a book that is overly short or overly long for its genre will incrementally decrease your odds of finding traditional publication and it may tip you over to the self-publishing world.

Word count is important in part due to the fact that paper books are a) placed in boxes and shipped around the world, b) placed on shelves, and c) often placed spine out. A book that is too short can literally be too narrow to have its spine out, and a book that is too long will crowd out others on the shelf, in addition to costing more coming and going due to the printing and distribution expenses.

I can hear your shouts …

"BUT WHAT ABOUT [FAMOUS BOOK] THAT IS [INSANELY LONG OR SHORT]"

Yes. Sure. There are exceptions.

But bear in mind that **most incredibly long and incredibly short books are not debuts.** J.K. Rowling started with two books of relatively conventional length before she had the latitude to start busting word count limits in the *Harry Potter* series. Vikram Seth was already a name before *A Suitable Boy*.

With self-publishing, you have more flexibility, so if you have a very long or very short novel, you may wish to consider it more seriously. (Although do bear in mind that you might still find your readers chafing at a novel that *feels* too long or too short.)

There are no hard and fast rules when it comes to word counts, and different sources are going to tell you different things. But overall, here's my own rough stab at word counts by genre:

Fiction
- Chapter Books (i.e., pre-Middle −Grade): 5,000–20,000
- Fantasy: 80,000–120,000
- General Fiction: 75,000–100,000
- Historical Fiction: 80,000–120,000
- Literary Fiction: 50,000–120,000
- Middle Grade: 30,000–60,000
- Mystery: 75,000–90,000
- Novella: 20,000–40,000
- Romance: 50,000–90,000
- Science Fiction: 90,000–120,000
- Thriller: 80,000–100,000
- Young Adult: 60,000–80,000

Nonfiction
- Biography: 80,000–120,000
- General Nonfiction: 75,000–100,000
- Memoir: 50,000–90,000
- Other Narrative Nonfiction: 80,000–120,000
- Self-Help: 40,000–80,000

3) HOW MUCH CONTROL DO YOU WANT OVER THE PUBLISHING PROCESS?

If you go the traditional route, you'll have an agent who will likely want you to edit your work before submission. You will (hopefully) have a publisher who will want you to revise your work. You probably won't have approval over your cover, and you'll probably only have mutual consent on your book title, meaning if your publisher doesn't like it, you'll have to think of a new one that you can both agree upon. You'll probably have limited control over how and where your book is marketed.

Traditional publishing (and often hybrid publishing) is a group process, and you absolutely cede some control over your book. This can be a good thing because chances are you're dealing with experienced people within the publishing industry who are experts in their fields, but you may be frustrated at times with decisions you don't agree with.

Meanwhile, with self-publishing, everything is up to you. Edits, cover, title, fonts, marketing, whether or not you want to include that stream of consciousness sequence about the philosophical implications of cotton candy ... all your choice.

4) HOW MUCH DOES THE VALIDATION OF TRADITIONAL PUBLISHING MATTER TO YOU?

The stigma surrounding self-publishing has largely dissipated, but it's not gone entirely.

For literary works in particular, garnering attention for awards and reviews is still pretty difficult outside of traditional publishing.

And there's still something gratifying about doing something as hugely difficult as making it through the traditional publishing process, having your work endorsed by professionals, and being paid for your efforts. The names Penguin Random House, HarperCollins, and Simon & Schuster ... they still matter to many people. Some hybrid publishers, such as Greenleaf, are also developing a name for themselves.

Success is success, and in the end it's the readers who are the ultimate validators. But be honest with yourself: Do you want the cachet that comes with traditional publishing? Or are you cool going straight to readers?

5) HOW IMPORTANT IS IT FOR YOUR BOOK TO BE IN BOOKSTORES AND LIBRARIES?

While you might be able to strike up some individual relationships with local bookstores and libraries as a self-published author, the surest route to bookstores and libraries on a national level is through traditional publishers, who have wide distribution. Perhaps the most crucial benefit that traditional publishers offer authors is that they are really good at getting books into bookstores.

Do you care about being in bookstores? Are you writing in a genre, like books for children, where libraries are super important?

If so, you might want to pursue traditional publication. Some of the more selective hybrid publishers also offer enhanced distribution, but do some research to verify the accuracy of their claims.

6) HOW CAPABLE ARE YOU AT MARKETING AND SELF-PROMOTION?

There's no guarantee that a traditional publisher is going to adequately promote your book, but they'll at least give you a bit of a boost, even at bare minimum. Hybrid publishers are a bit spottier, but the good ones will also do what they can to get the word out.

If you self-publish, you're entirely on your own. You don't necessarily have to be a social media maven or a celebrity in order to give your book the boost necessary to generate crucial word of mouth, but you're going to have to do *something*.

(More on what these marketing efforts can look like in Rule #36.)

7) CAN YOU AFFORD TO INVEST MONEY IN YOUR BOOK?

Say what you will about traditional publishing, but one great thing about it is that it is not very cost prohibitive. You might incur some postage sending your manuscript around or if you choose to pay an editor before pursuing publication, but agents don't charge you until they get their commission for selling your book, and publishers pay you while they incur the cost of getting the book out there.

Self-publishing doesn't have to be hugely cost-prohibitive, but there are a lot of tasks involved in self-publishing, such as generating a cover, editing, copyediting, formatting, and marketing, that you're either going to have to spend the time to do yourself or pay someone to do for you.

Depending on how much time you have to spend and your level of expertise, you may end up spending several thousand dollars to effectively self-publish and potentially more if you choose to do paid marketing. (See Rule #26 for more on the economics of self-publishing.)

Can you afford this? (And you shouldn't necessarily assume you're going to earn it back.)

Meanwhile, there are really two types of authors who should consider hybrid publishing: Authors with cash who are looking for a bit more upside than regular self-publishing and authors with cash who don't want to manage the publishing process on their own. Notice the "with cash" part? Yeah. If you don't have cash to burn, traditional and self-publishing are the more economical ways of getting your book out there.

8) HOW PATIENT ARE YOU?

Choosing between traditional, self-publishing, and hybrid publishing isn't necessarily an either/or decision. You can absolutely decide to pursue traditional publishing first and fall back on self-publishing or hybrid publishing if you so desire.

But even in the best-case scenario, traditional publishing can take forever. It can take a year or more to query agents, and then a few months up to a year or more to find an editor when you're on submission to publishers, and even if you then get a book deal, it can be a year or two after that before your book comes out. It can very easily add up to two or three years or more after you finish your manuscript.

Meanwhile, when I finished *How to Write a Novel*, I was able to get it up for sale a few days later. Self-publishing is practically instantaneous.

Are you the patient type? Do you want to cut to the chase? This can be the most important factor of all.

WHAT TO DO NEXT

If you've decided to try your luck with traditional publishing, keep on reading! Proceed directly to the next rule and start to learn how the process works.

If hybrid publishing sounds like your cup of tea, familiarize yourself with how to write a query letter (Rules #12-15), research the submission requirements for the hybrid publishers that you're interested in, and then go ahead and submit. If they want to work with you, make sure you know what you're signing (Rules #21 and #22 can be helpful).

Ready to self-publish? Head on over to Rule #26.

And if you're still unsure? Just go ahead and read the whole darn book and then see how you feel.

ALL ABOUT TRADITIONAL PUBLISHING

Rule #7
UNDERSTAND WHAT LITERARY AGENTS DO

Literary agents fulfill a crucial role in the traditional publishing process and their responsibilities touch on nearly every facet of the path to publication.

So let's examine these different hats, shall we? Behold! This chapter is organized by tracking one book project from a query letter to what happens after a book is sold, looking at all the things your agent will do along the way.

THE LITERARY AGENT FILTER

Literary agents are the baleen to the publishing industry's whale. The Brita to the publishing industry's drinking water. The pan to the publishing industry's gold. (I could go on.)

Basically: agents serve as a filter. Literary agents comb through all of those potential book projects and present editors with only the very best ones.

This means that agents open the floodgates to submissions. Most agents receive between 5,000 and 20,000 or more submissions a year and choose only a few carefully selected projects to send to editors. They may also think of book ideas on top of these submissions and then try to source potential authors.

Agents may specialize in certain areas or they may be generalists, but they all have to reject way way way more projects than they are able to take on.

PRE-SUBMISSION EDITING

Because the marketplace is so competitive, many agents will work with clients or prospective clients on their manuscripts or proposals prior to submission to publishers to ensure the project has its very best chance to catch an editor's eye.

I was a hands-on agent and would often work with authors on revisions before offering representation so that we could both get a sense of how well we would work together. It also gave me a sense of how well that writer could take edits and feedback, which is such a central part of the process.

A project has to be as perfect as possible in order to attract an editor, so it behooves both agent and author to work together to improve the project or proposal before it goes on submission.

SUBMITTING TO EDITORS

Submitting a project to editors is both an art and a science.

The science: a huge part of being an agent involves networking, knowing which editors like what type of books, networking, keeping imprints and mergers and layoffs and new hires straight, networking, keeping up with industry news and gossip, networking, and networking.

The art: an agent will write a carefully crafted pitch letter to help "sell" the book and select the best editors to consider a particular project, but at the end of the day an agent never quite knows who is going to respond most positively to a particular project.

Then agents will also pester the editors they submitted to at regular intervals until they get a response.

Also, it's worth mentioning that every responsibility I've listed up until this point is done on spec—an agent has not yet been paid for any of this. Since agents only receive income if they're able to sell a project, they could very well spend tens to hundreds of hours on a project, send it to editors, and end up with $0 to show for their efforts.

NEGOTIATING OFFERS AND PUBLISHING CONTRACTS

Hooray! An offer comes in!

Now the agent will help you decide what comes next. There are different types of offers with different rights, territories, and terms, and, of course, the dollar amounts of advances vary greatly. It's an agent's job to negotiate the terms of the offer upward, possibly conduct an auction if multiple houses are interested, and make sure the i's are crossed and the t's are dotted before you accept.

This, along with the submission process, is really where an agent earns their 15%. Good agents know how to negotiate, they know how to get the best terms, and they know which rights to grant publishers and which ones to hold onto.

Some agencies have in-house contract specialists, and some have agents negotiate the contracts themselves. All will negotiate an agreement that is far, far better than what an unagented author would be able to achieve on their own.

KEEPING TRACK OF THE PUBLICATION PROCESS

An agent will follow up on payments and badger publishers until said payments come in, keep track of key dates, discuss marketing plans with you and your editor, serve as a mediator between you and the publisher in the case of any disputes arising, and generally keep on top of everything to make sure everything is proceeding as it should.

SELLING SUBRIGHTS

Remember during the offer stage when the agent and publisher were negotiating the terms of the offer and contract? The agent may have been able to hold onto some of the rights, such as film, audio, and translation, which can be sold directly to other publishers and studios. These rights can be quite lucrative, and if they're sold directly you don't have to split the revenue with the publisher.

Some agencies work with subagents to place these rights, while others have in-house film and foreign rights departments. These rights can add up to significant additional income for you.

CAREER GUIDANCE

Even apart from the nuts and bolts tasks that go into making an individual book happen, an agent can help you plan your career trajectory, whether this involves helping you choose projects to pursue, thinking of new ideas for breaking you out to larger audiences, serving as a sounding board, brainstorming, keeping you apprised of changes in the industry, and in general providing an experienced ear and brain, helping you to navigate the business.

Ultimately: the agent is your advocate. They help you become more successful and will work tirelessly to advance your career.

This is just a basic list, and there's often more to it than this. It's quite a catchall job, one that requires a long apprenticeship, a strong work ethic, a thick skin, a good eye, and a passion for books.

For all of these tasks, the agent receives income based only on commission—again, the agent is only paid if/when you are paid.

But a good agent is seriously worth their weight in gold.

So how do you nab yourself one of these elusive, helpful creatures?

I'll get to that in a jiffy.

Rule #8
PRACTICE GOOD ETIQUETTE DURING YOUR SEARCH

Before I get into the heart of this field guide to finding and interacting with the rare and colorful species *Literarius Agentia*, known popularly as "literary agents," allow me first to get this out of the way:

No one is going to reject you solely because of a mild faux pas.

Don't let this guide to literary agent etiquette result in crippling paranoia. Try to get things right and do your best to know what's customary, but don't sweat it too much at the end of the day. If you're generally ethical, well-intentioned, and diligent, you'll be fine.

These aren't hard and fast rules, just what is customary from one veteran's perspective. It increases your odds to know the customs of the business and act professionally. Think of a literary agent like a venture capitalist and you're pitching a business plan. You're asking someone to invest their time and money in your book in the hope that it's an eventual success.

Would you honestly go into a pitch meeting with a V.C. with no idea whatsoever how these normally work and a shoddy business plan?

(Well. Maybe you would. But don't.)

Here are some dos, don'ts, and FAQs:

DO: FOLLOW SUBMISSION GUIDELINES

In order to find a literary agent, you're almost assuredly going to need to approach literary agents with a query letter, which is an incredibly important missive that describes your book and, if applicable, your qualifications. These letters are now usually handled via email, but some literary agents use automated services and others still want you to send them through the postal service the old fashioned way. (More on query letters in Rule #12.)

No matter what you see in this guide or elsewhere around the internet, an agent's submission guidelines trump everything. As you're researching literary agents, make a note of how they want to be approached and then ... just do that.

Seriously. Follow them.

DON'T: CONTACT AN AGENT ASKING IF IT'S OKAY TO SEND THEM A QUERY LETTER

When I was a literary agent, I used to get tons of query letters from people asking me if it was okay to send me a query letter.

Yes. You heard correctly. A query letter to see if it's okay to send a query letter.

Don't ask. Just send. Even if you can't find their submission guidelines online.

DO: POLISH YOUR MANUSCRIPT (FICTION/MEMOIRS) OR PROPOSAL (NONFICTION) BEFORE YOU SUBMIT TO A LITERARY AGENT

You might be wondering: Can I query if I'm an unpublished author and my book isn't finished just to test out the idea?

No.

DON'T: COLD CALL AN AGENT OR SWING BY TO DROP OFF AN UNSOLICITED SUBMISSION

You will only succeed in annoying them. And possibly terrifying them.

DO: REMEMBER THAT AGENTS ARE BUSY

Authors who have spent months or years on a manuscript and feel emotionally invested in their work tend to feel like they are *owed* a personalized, detailed response from a prospective literary agent, even if it's just a query.

This just isn't how it works. They're not going to give you free query tips, suggestions for other agents to try, career advice, or clues for finding Willy Wonka's golden ticket.

Literary agents are not an information booth. Rejecting manuscripts and responding to prospective clients' questions is not how agents make their living. They make their living selling book projects to publishers.

FAQ: CAN I SUBMIT TO MULTIPLE AGENTS AT THE SAME AGENCY?

Unless otherwise specified in the submission guidelines, it's fine to query different agents at the same agency, as long as each agent represents your genre.

However, in order to avoid conflicts, I'd highly recommend querying only one agent at a particular agency at a given time and waiting a bit after receiving a rejection before trying another agent. Sometimes agents share assistants who do the first pass reading queries. It's best if they're not seeing the query again first thing after they just sent a rejection.

FAQ: WHEN SHOULD I TELL A LITERARY AGENT ABOUT [THIS ONE THING THAT I'M WONDERING ABOUT]?

When you're approaching literary agents, it can be tricky to know when the appropriate time might be to discuss manuscripts in the drawer, other offers, or your absolutely true alien encounters.

Here's a rough guide for when to give an agent a heads-up about a nubby situation:

- **You had a previous agent** – I'd mention this in the query. It shows that someone had invested in your work, even if it didn't work out for whatever reason.
- **You're writing under a pen name** – Query as your real name, but feel free to mention the pen name if you want to.
- **Editor(s) at a publisher are considering your manuscript** – Mention this in the query.
- **You are previously published or self-published** – Mention this in the query and specify the publishers and dates.
- **Your age** – If you're under 18, mention this in the query. Otherwise, there's no need to mention this.
- **The other book projects you have in the drawer** – Wait until you receive an offer of representation, then discuss how the agent would like to approach these.

A good rule of thumb for anything I didn't cover above: If the information is relevant to the particular project you're querying about, mention it in the query.

If it's a general question about your career, wait until the agent expresses interest in your current project.

FAQ: WHEN SHOULD I FOLLOW UP WITH A LITERARY AGENT?

Contrary to popular belief among some fearful authors, literary agents will not be scared off and disappear into an angry puff of smoke the moment you send them a follow-up email.

An agent's inbox looks like the electronic equivalent of Niagara Falls, and at any given time they will have literally thousands of pages in their to-be-read pile. As a result, most agents will appreciate a timely and extremely polite nudge. (If they would get annoyed by one, would you really want to work with them anyway?)

Bear in mind that the below are just rules of thumb and different agents are always going to feel differently. An individual agent's stated preferences always win for that agent.

Here's my advice on agent communication and follow ups:

- **Following up on query letters** – Unless otherwise specified by the agent, it's not customary to follow up on query letters. Many agents have "no reply means no" policies, and they will get annoyed pretty fast if you start chasing after a query that they didn't reply to. Yes, I know, it's really scary to think your query got lost in the ether and was never seen by your dream agent, but that's the way the e-cookie crumbles. The only exception to this is if the agent specifically requested a query letter from you in a referral situation or where there's some sort of a personal connection. In this case, I'd wait a few weeks and check again.

- **Following up on partial and full manuscript requests** – If an agent requests a partial or full manuscript from you, they will *expect* you to follow up at some point if they haven't gotten back to you in a timely fashion. I recommend following up once after six weeks and once a month thereafter until you either hear back or get tired of following up.

- **When you receive an offer of representation** – If you receive an offer of representation, it's customary to then follow up with all the agents who are currently considering your manuscript, whether it's a partial or a full. Give them a reasonable timeframe (7–14 days) to get back to you so that you don't leave the agent who offered you representation hanging. Opinions vary somewhat on whether to follow up with agents who only have your query letter, but if you have a dream agent on your list, it's not going to kill your chances to follow up with them. I wouldn't advise sending out new queries. (More on how to handle an offer of representation in Rule #19.)

When you send follow ups, remember: agents are busy.

You have one manuscript to worry about. Agents are juggling dozens. Try to remember that the nature of the job is hectic and don't let your impatience get the best of you.

Whenever you follow up with an agent, always be exceedingly polite, reply to your existing thread of conversation with the agent so they can easily see your previous correspondence, and give them all the context they need to easily respond to your message (e.g., if you're following up on a manuscript, re-attach the manuscript).

FAQ: CAN I RE-QUERY AN AGENT?

If an agent passed on your query, I wouldn't re-query them with the same project again barring some major revision that ended up in it essentially being a different book. When I was an agent, I didn't reconsider something I'd already passed on because it was enough work to keep up with all the first-time queries and manuscripts, let alone all the ones that would have flooded in if I considered revisions.

That said, after you've completed a very extensive revision, I don't see the harm in explaining that you revised the material and feel the work is much stronger, that you appreciate their time, and that you wonder if they'd take another look. At worst they're just going to say no, but who knows, maybe they'll be persuaded to look again.

If the agent passed on your work but specifically asked for revisions, they are *expecting* to hear from you again.

If you want to query an agent with a totally new project, I would wait a few months before querying them if they recently passed on your earlier project. There are few things more annoying for an agent than passing on one project only to receive an e-mail five minutes later saying, "Okay, what about this one?" and, after that one is rejected, receiving another one that says, "Okay, what about this one?" (This happened enough when I was agent that I didn't even respond to the follow-up query. I couldn't bear to get myself into a game of "what about this one?")

FAQ: AN AGENT ASKED TO CONSIDER MY MANU-SCRIPT/PROPOSAL "EXCLUSIVELY." WHAT DOES THAT MEAN?

When an agent likes your query and wants to consider your manuscript, they may request an "exclusive." This means what it sounds like. You are giving the agent the opportunity to consider your work exclusively, and you are agreeing that you will not submit to another agent until you've heard "yea" or "nay" from that agent. Sometimes exclusives are open-ended (though I would advise that you avoid these like the plague), and sometimes there's a time period attached.

Granting an exclusive look does not preclude you from continuing to query other agents, although it does mean that you have to put any agents who ask for your book on hold until the period of exclusivity is up. You also can't grant an exclusive if another agent is already considering your manuscript/proposal.

Agents mainly ask for them so they don't have to worry about having an author swept out from under them and the time they're spent reading the manuscript/proposal wasted. However, they aren't always advantageous for an author because they can limit an author's choice and stall the process. Be selective about how you grant exclusives (you're within your rights to say no), and whatever you do make sure there's a time limit. Thirty days is a reasonable time period for an agent to consider a partial or full exclusively, after which you should feel free to send your manuscript to any agents who have inquired in the meantime.

If the agent has read your manuscript or proposal and is offering to work with you exclusively on editing it, this is something different that I shall cover in Rule #18.

FAQ: UM ... THIS SEEMS LIKE A LOT TO REMEMBER?

Yes, there is a lot to keep track of.

But remember: just do your best. If you're going about this process with respect, transparency, and good intentions, you will be fine.

Rule #9
KNOW YOUR RIGHTS AND WATCH OUT FOR BAD AGENTS

Be careful out there.

Many aspiring authors feel that all they have to do is write a good book, sit back, and let the god of easy publishing deals take care of the rest. Not so! Before you embark on your quest for a literary agent, you should devote many, many hours familiarizing yourself with the business, literary agents, editors, and anything else you can possibly do to discern how this unique industry operates. Luckily, there is more information out there on the internet than ever before, and you are doing well by reading this guide right now.

Treat this business seriously because it *is* a business. Read blogs, talk to booksellers, attend conferences, and get to know authors. If you do this *before* you try to find an agent, your odds of success will increase dramatically because you will ooze professionalism and knowledge, qualities that bode well for future successful writers.

While the internet has been an incredible boon to authors and there's more information about how to navigate the publishing process than ever before, there has also been an explosion of scammers who may try to prey on your dreams.

Protecting yourself starts with good research and knowing your rights as an author. Here are some key things to know.

LITERARY AGENTS ONLY GET PAID WHEN YOU GET PAID

It should not cost you anything to have your work read by an agent. Once more with feeling: reputable agents work on commission, meaning they take 15% of an author's advance or royalties in exchange for their services (20% for overseas rights). There should not be any reading fees or consulting fees or anything else charged to you. Especially things you didn't know about in advance.

They also shouldn't be upselling you on services or immediately landing you a "publisher" who wants you to "invest" in getting your book out there. These are big red flags.

A GOOD AGENT SHOULD ADHERE TO THE AAR'S CANON OF ETHICS

The Association of Authors' Representatives (AAR) is an organization that vets its membership and ensures that all of its agents adhere to a canon of ethics. Not all reputable agents are members of the AAR, so don't disqualify an agent just because they're not one, but if you are approaching a member of the AAR, you can feel more confident that they are reputable. The AAR has a database you can search on their website.

But really, any reputable agent should adhere to the standards set by the AAR. Here's an abridged version of the AAR's Canon of Ethics:

- Agents are loyal to their clients' business, avoid conflicts of interest, and never deceive or defraud their clients, other agents, the general public, or anyone else with whom they do business.
- Agents are responsible and secure with their clients' funds. Payments must be made on time. Books of account must be open.
- Agents may pass along charges, such as photocopies and purchase of books used for sales of other rights.

- Agents keep their clients apprised of matters entrusted to them and provide information that the clients request.
- Agents cannot represent both the buyer and seller in a transaction.
- Agents may not receive a secret profit and may not receive a referral fee.
- Agents keep their clients' financial information confidential.
- Agents may not charge clients or potential clients reading fees.

YOUR WORK IS PROTECTED EVEN IF YOU DON'T FILE FOR COPYRIGHT WITH THE LIBRARY OF CONGRESS

There's a common misconception that authors need to file their work with the Library of Congress and/or put a copyright symbol on their manuscript in order to protect it.

Neither is true. You own your copyright the second your work is produced. Registering copyright with the Library of Congress confers additional benefits, but it's usually not advisable to register for copyright until/unless the book is published. If you have a traditional publisher, they typically handle this for you.

(Please do not construe this as legal advice. Consult with a publishing attorney if you are unsure about your rights.)

BE WARY OF ANYONE TRYING TO "UPSELL" YOU SERVICES OR WHO APPROACHES YOU OUT OF THE BLUE

Now, let me be clear that good and reputable literary agents and editors will absolutely reach out to people proactively to see whether they have representation or might be interested in writing a book.

But if someone approaches you out of the blue with a "book deal" where you have to pay a share of the printing costs or they try to get you to buy additional services, like marketing, be very, very careful. Do your research on the people you're thinking of working with and make sure you're clear about how the traditional publishing process and self-publishing process are supposed to work.

There are great freelance publishing professionals out there who can help you, but make sure you're always doing your due diligence.

FAMILIARIZE YOURSELF WITH REPUTABLE RESOURCES FOR AUTHORS

There are some great, honest experts on the internet who want to help steer authors in the right direction. Here are some valuable resources:

- **Association of Authors' Representatives**
  – As mentioned earlier in the chapter, this is a good place to locate agents who adhere to the AAR's canon of ethics.

- **Writer Beware at SFWA and the Writer Beware blog** – A great resource for spotting scams and learning more about what's customary within the business.
- **Absolute Write message boards** – A large community of writers dedicated to helping other writers and swapping knowledge.
- **Me** – My blog (blog.nathanbransford.com) has a ton of resources on navigating the publishing process. And if you ever have any questions, please reach out to me directly and I'll do my best to help (nathan@nathanbransford.com). I can't guarantee I'll be able to help everyone, but I'll do my best to steer you in the right direction!

LEARN TO SPOT BAD (AND FAKE) AGENTS

Some literary agents are fantastic. They worked their way up through an apprenticeship process and toiled hard working for an established agent before they knew the business well enough to take on clients. When they started taking on their own projects, they were prepared. Now they have lots of sales to major publishers under their belts.

Others just hung out a shingle. Maybe they had some connection to the business, maybe it was just a life-long dream, maybe they're a writer who got fed up and decided if you can't beat 'em, become one. Maybe they have even managed to sell a few books.

The hardest thing: some agents who don't know what they're doing don't even know they don't know what they're doing. They may have the best intentions, they may be hard-working people, but there's a lot more to being an agent than knowing how to read a contract or possessing a rolodex.

Make sure the agent who wants to represent you is legit. **Your best bet is to find either an established agent who has a substantial track record selling books to the Big 5 publishers or young agents who have put in a few years apprenticing for established agents.**

Every agent starts with zero sales, and sometimes young agents can be a good fit because they're hungry and actively looking to build their list. Make sure a young agent has spent at least a few years learning the ropes from someone who really knows what they're doing. For instance, by the time I started taking on clients, I had worked at Curtis Brown Ltd. for over two years, had an entire office of veterans I could draw upon if I ever had any questions, had sold audio and other subsidiary rights for bestselling authors, and had already worked with some of the biggest names in the business.

BEWARE OF "SPAGHETTI AGENTS"

As you're searching, try to sniff out spaghetti agents.

What's a spaghetti agent? Well, it's a term I made up. Basically, you know that phrase about throwing spaghetti against the wall to see what sticks?

That's a spaghetti agent. They sign up a bunch of writers even when they're unsure about a project, they throw the manuscripts at publishers, and they see what sticks.

On the one hand, this isn't actually the worst strategy in the world. As much as people would like to think that agents are clairvoyant, at the end of the day you never really know what's going to resonate with publishers. So spaghetti agents are acknowledging this fact and are spreading their odds across a lot of different projects.

The problem for writers is that since spaghetti agents will send out projects even when they might be on the fence, they may be sending out projects that aren't quite ready. And in a competitive publishing landscape, it pays for a project to be as ready as humanly possible. Spaghetti agents may also have a shaky reputation with editors because they send out so much stuff and it's not always of the highest quality.

Back when I was an agent, I can't tell you how many times I would find a manuscript that was close but not quite ready and wanted to work with the writer on a revision, only to be undercut by a spaghetti agent. I would offer to work with the author on a revision, the author would say they had an offer of representation on the table, and then I'd be in a bind. I couldn't really guarantee that I'd take on the project without seeing the revision, and I also couldn't very well advise an author to give up the bird in the hand when they had someone else who seemed enthusiastic about their work. So, I'd stand aside and let the author go. A few times this worked out for the author, but quite a few times it didn't.

What can you do as an author?

When you're offered representation, ask good questions. Ask how long they're willing to keep your work on submission. Are they just going to try with the big publishers or are they considering small presses? It's an important question because one hallmark of a spaghetti agent is submitting and dashing. They'll send a project out to a few editors, gauge the response, and then bolt if it's not working quickly. Not every good agent is willing to keep something on submission endlessly, so don't put *too* much stock in this question, but make sure you're comfortable with the answer. (See Rule #19 for more on handling an offer of representation.)

If you're getting multiple responses of "I like this but don't know if it's quite ready" from some agents, but then one wants to go out with it immediately ... take a long pause and really, really think it through. I'm not necessarily advising giving up the bird in the hand, or advising you to feel paranoid, because this may just be the one agent who really gets your work, and they might be completely right in feeling that it's ready to go. Just make sure it's the right choice. After all, having the wrong agent can be worse than having no agent at all.

After working so long on your book and wanting so badly to go out on submission, it's tempting to want to leap into the arms of the first agent who will have you. But be sure and take your time, do your research, and make sure it's the right fit before proceeding. Otherwise, your manuscript could get thrown against the publishing wall before it's ready, and you only get one chance to see if it sticks.

Rule #10
NONFICTION WRITERS, YOU NEED TO WRITE A PROPOSAL

If you're seeking traditional publication for a nonfiction book, you're almost assuredly going to need to write a nonfiction book proposal. (The main exception is memoir, which, if you're not already famous, tends to work a bit more like novels, meaning you'll probably need to write the entire thing.)

Why a proposal for nonfiction? A literary agent can often sell nonfiction projects on proposal, meaning you write the proposal first, then sell the project, and then write the book. It mostly depends on the quality of the idea and its marketability, your platform (a combination of your credentials and ability to promote the book), and your writing ability.

"Whoops!" some of you are thinking, "I wish I had known this because I already wrote the book."

Yeah ... sorry about that. It's fine to pitch agents with a nonfiction manuscript, but an agent may still end up wanting you to write a book proposal to submit to editors.

Book proposals focus on what literary agent Mitchell Waters refers to as the "The Four C's: Concept, Credentials, Consumers, and Craft."

So how do you go about writing a proposal? Well, writing a nonfiction book proposal is sort of like cooking lasagna. There are a thousand ways of making it and everyone has their own recipe, but almost every lasagna has a few basic ingredients and chances are it's going to taste good in the end. The below recipe, if you will, applies to just about every kind of nonfiction, from history to self-help to narrative nonfiction.

Here are the basic sections of a nonfiction book proposal.

OVERVIEW

The overview is typically a page or two that gives, well, an overview of the book you plan to write. You're getting across the meat of the topic that you are writing about, in the case of narrative nonfiction, or the challenge you're helping people to solve in the case of prescriptive projects. It's really a sales pitch.

A good overview (also sometimes called an "introduction") will give the agent/editor a strong sense of the subject, the scope, the heart of the project, and the need for the book. It will get them excited about what you're going to write.

Although the overview isn't an actual excerpt from the book, try to infuse it with the writing style you plan to employ for the eventual book. Agents and editors should have a sense of what it would be like to read the book. It should have a cohesive and authoritative voice.

In the words of literary agent Tess Callero: "The key to nailing an introduction is storytelling. Tell me who you are and why you are the person who should be writing this book, but in a way that gives me access to your world and immerses me in the story."

If you're stuck, check out the jacket copy for books that are similar to yours and see the way the books are framed. An overview won't be exactly like jacket copy (remember you're pitching an agent/editor, not a reader), but it's a good starting place for laying out the scope of your book.

AUTHOR'S BIO

Your bio is how you introduce yourself to agents and give them a sense of your qualifications and experience. There are looking for two primary things.

- **Your credentials to write this book.** Are you among the world's foremost experts in your field? Have you published articles in national publications on your topic that generated substantial interest?
- **Your ability to draw an audience.** Do you have an existing audience base, can you be booked on television shows, do you have a social media following or a substantial mailing list, or do you have connections in your field that could be helpful to draw upon?

Note that you don't necessarily have to have previous publishing credits, but they can certainly be helpful in giving agents and editors a sense of your writing style and your ability to engage readers.

A bio in a book proposal is usually three or four paragraphs long, no more than a page, so don't go overboard here and include every detail in your entire life history.

COMPETING OR COMPARATIVE ("COMP") TITLES/ MARKET ANALYSIS

Competing or comparative titles refers to a list of 7–10 books that are similar to yours or could be viewed as competitive or as evidence of a potentially receptive audience for a similar book. The goal with this section is to establish that there's a market for your book, you will address a gap in this market, and your book is unlike the other books out there.

For each comp title you'll need a quick summary of the book, how well it sold (if you're able to determine this), and how your book is different.

Of these three items, how well it performed is the least important to include, and at the stage where you're trying to find an agent you don't really need much beyond including whether it was a bestseller or not. An agent will likely have access to Bookscan (a service that approximates overall book sales) and can help flesh out sales performance if they feel it's important to be specific before the proposal goes out to publishers.

OUTLINE/LIST OF CHAPTERS

Sometimes people include an outline or a list of chapters to give a sense of the scope of the project, along with descriptions of what the chapters cover. It's another way of helping an agent or editor envision what the finished book would be like.

Personally, I feel like this part is a little overrated for something like narrative nonfiction because the finished product is probably going to change, but this section is very important for any sort of self-help-ish or business-ish proposal since you should already have a pretty good idea of where the project is going and can summarize it here.

ONE TO THREE SAMPLE CHAPTERS

Other than perhaps the overview, the sample is the most important part of the proposal. Some editors I know just get a gist of the overview and then turn straight to the sample chapters to see the author's writing. So work very, very hard on these chapters to make them as good as possible.

You'll want to include about 25–50 pages so the agent and editor can get a sense of your writing ability.

OTHER

Some agents may ask for a marketing summary that includes what you would be able to do to promote the book. This may include any blurbs/quotes from prominent people that the publisher could slap on the jacket copy, if you have them, as well as anything else that could give a sense of your ability to help market the book.

Other things that you might consider including in a proposal are copies of newspaper/magazine articles you wrote that relate to the subject of the book, (good) reviews of past nonfiction books you've published, and anything else that will help convince the agent/ editor that you're super awesome.

And that's pretty much it! Easy as lasagna.

RESEARCH PROSPECTIVE AGENTS

There are hundreds of agents out there. Some are incredibly powerful and can transform your destiny with a few emails. Some, as we recently discussed, are scam artists (knowingly or unknowingly). So how can you tell the difference? How do you figure out who you can trust?

Here is how to go about researching agents and compiling a target list for querying.

Before you start the search, make sure you know the goals of your research:

- You want to create a list of reputable agents who represent your genre and get a sense of which ones you most want to work with.
- You want to know their submission guidelines and contact information so you can then query them according to their exact specifications.
- You want to personalize your query, so keep track of tidbits you can use in your query. (Think: "I chose to query you because I'm a huge fan of [Author agent has represented]" or "Anyone who has trained their goldfish to do tricks is fine by me.")

Consider tracking all of this in a spreadsheet so that you can refer to it later and rank your prospective agents.

Now then, on to the search!

KNOW (AND BE HONEST ABOUT) YOUR GENRE

Agents specialize. While they have some flexibility and autonomy around what they represent, they almost all have certain genres they do and don't represent.

Specializing allows agents to focus their networking on the editors and publishers that acquire certain genres. It's hard to keep track of genre conventions, trends, and personnel for every single genre out there. Agents tend to have a better "eye" for certain genres than others. For instance, when I was an agent, I had a really hard time spotting good picture books, so I didn't represent them. And ultimately, it's more enjoyable to specialize in genres you personally like.

As you know from Rule #5, you should know the genre of your work before you begin.

START IN THE OBVIOUS PLACES

Okay. So. You have your genre, and you're ready to start. There are two good starting places.

First, try to find out who represents your favorite authors in your genre. You can use the ol' Google for this one; otherwise, a good place to look is in the acknowledgments sections of books. The only exception to this is that you may want to avoid agents who represent something *too* similar to your work. Same genre? Cool. Eerily similar plot line? Might want to steer clear.

You can also ask the people you know who have agents or who are connected to the publishing industry for recommendations (and by "people you know" I mean "people you actually know in real life who are familiar with your work").

See if you can compile an initial list of names and see if you can secure a referral, which is one of the best ways to find an agent. As with anything in life, it's helpful to know people who know people. For many of the more experienced/legendary agents, referrals are darn near essential because the agents may have closed their doors to unsolicited submissions.

If you don't have preexisting personal connections, the best ways to garner a referral are to get involved with online and offline writers' communities, fraternize with writers, interact with writers on social media, and put yourself in a position where your work will be seen by other established writers. Genuinely (and not selfishly) invest in these writers and you may find that they will invest in you.

Now, notice that I didn't suggest the "e-mail random writers and ask for referrals out of the blue" approach, which has about a zero chance of success. These things have to evolve organically.

SUPPLEMENT YOUR RESEARCH WITH DATABASES

The agents who represent the books you love and who you've been recommended to may well comprise your initial "top tier" of agents. But you want to do more research than this.

There are a few databases out there that can help. All of them allow you to filter by genre:

- **Publishers Marketplace** – This is a great place to see the writers whom various agents represent and what projects the agent has sold. Many agents have created their own pages with lots of good information.

- **The AAR Database** – As mentioned in Rule #9, the AAR is a good place to look for reputable agents. All the agents abide by a canon of ethics and have to meet certain criteria for membership. Not all ethical agents are members of the AAR, but the agents in the AAR should be legit.
- **Agent Query** and **Query Tracker** – These sites will allow you to cast a wider net, but you'll definitely want to supplement your research to make sure the people you're finding are reputable.

Combing through these should give you a long list of people to query. Next you want to start winnowing down your list.

CONFIRM AN AGENT'S BONA FIDES

So. You now have a list of 100 or so agents you could potentially query. How do you know they're real? Better yet, how do you know if they're right for you and your unique book?

Make sure you read Rule #9 very carefully and that you know your rights as an author. Learn to spot major red flags. Check their sales records and make sure they have placed books with major publishers or work for an established agent.

PRIORITIZE

How should you rank your top prospective agents, the people you will query first? Go with your gut.

Get a feel for the books an agent represents. Follow them on social media and get a sense of their personality. Rank your list. You can't know in advance who the perfect agent will be, and don't get your heart set on any one agent, but you can get in the ballpark by getting a sense of whether you think you'd enjoy working with them.

Good research can help you find the agent of your dreams and stave off the disaster of ending up with a bad one.

Rule #12
WRITE A KILLER QUERY LETTER

A query letter is part business letter, part creative writing exercise, part introduction, and part death-defying leap through a flaming hoop. (Don't worry, you won't catch fire and die during the query process, though it may feel precisely like this at times.)

In essence, it is a letter describing your project. But it is so much more than this.

The first thing to know about writing a query letter is that there are as many opinions out there on the internet about query letters as there are, well, opinions on the internet. You will find lots of dos and don'ts and pet peeves and strategies and formulas. The important thing to remember about this is that everyone is wrong except for me. (Just kidding. The important thing to remember is that you will need to choose the ideas that work best for you.)

As the immortal Douglas Adams said, don't panic! Write the best query letter you can, be yourself, don't overthink it too much, don't sweat it if you realize the second after you sent it that you made a typo or accidentally called an agent Vicky when their name is Bartholomew. If an agent is going to get mad or reject you over something trivial like this, they're probably not the type of person you'd want to work with anyway.

Clear eyes, full hearts, can't lose.

RESEARCH AND PERSONALIZE!

Make your query letter shine through personalization. To do this, as we discussed in the previous rule, you need to research literary agents so that you can show them you queried them individually.

Lots of authors feel queasy about personalizing their queries. If the book is all that matters, why do they have to jump through the hoop of sending dozens of individualized queries?

The reason personalization works isn't because agents like being kissed up to. It's because it's a tipoff that the author has taken the time to do their research and is going about the process professionally. It's like that old Van Halen story about how they'd include something deep in their contract rider about having a bowl of M&Ms with all the brown ones removed in the backstage area. It wasn't to be prima donnas, it was an easy way to see if the venue paid attention to detail.

If you're researching the agent and adding a personalized touch, it shows you're taking the time to be a well-educated and well-prepared writer, which reflects well on your dedication to the craft and business of writing. It gets an agent's attention.

As you're personalizing, the first and easiest thing to do is to just get an agent's name right. When I was an agent, I kept track for a while and found that a full 23% of writers messed up my name, everything from "Dear Editor" to "Dear Vicky Bijur." Even if you're sending to a general email address, make sure to address your query to a specific person.

Once you've mastered the whole "spelling someone's name right" thing, it's time to work in that nugget of personalized information from your research. You don't need to go overboard on this or be a kissup, it can be something as simple as saying you enjoyed a book by one of their authors or saw an interview where they said something interesting. Don't be overly general, like saying you're querying them because they represent a particular genre; show you really researched them.

In short, be brief, be specific, don't fake it, and then get on to the rest of the query.

WRITE THE BODY OF YOUR PITCH

Ah, the fun part. Only not really.

You are in luck, as I have a handy dandy mad lib in Rule #13 to get you started. Just plug the details of your novel into the query letter template and it will give you a basic query letter to start with. From there, expand on it, personalize it, and make it your own. Also, draw upon the two paragraph pitch you hopefully decided to write after reading Rule #5.

You are trying to accomplish two important objectives with the query. You want to make the plot/subject of your book sound awesome and to show the agent that you write well.

Try as much as possible to write the query letter so that it embodies the spirit of your book. If your book is funny, write a funny a query letter. If your book is written with beautiful, lyrical prose, write your query letter accordingly.

For fiction, be as specific as possible about the plot rather than descending into generalities. (More on this in Rule #15.)

For nonfiction, it's very important to give a sense of your level of expertise, your platform, and how much publicity you could bring to bear in the promotion of your work.

INCLUDE A BRIEF BIO

If you're writing a novel and don't have a shred of publishing credits to your name, just use these magic words: "This is my first novel." (I didn't have any publishing credits before I found a literary agent.)

Otherwise, you should include all the books you have published and/or self-published, along with the publisher and year. This is important. Don't make the agent go hunting for who published them or when they were released.

As a general rule of thumb, only include non-book publishing credits if they're relevant to your book project. This means, if you're writing fiction, published short stories in reputable journals are relevant. Academic papers or unrelated articles in a magazine are not. Also, only include publishing credits that have at least a regional audience. Publishing a letter to the editor in your local paper isn't going to impress.

If you're writing nonfiction, you're going to want to give some thought to conveying your platform (remember: authority plus audience), but you don't need to include a super elaborate and detailed bio in the query letter. Just focus on giving a sense of your credibility on the topic and any marketing activities you would be able to bring to bear.

It's totally okay for authors of all stripes to tell the agent a bit about themselves in their query letter, like what they do for a living or a quirky tidbit. This can give more of a sense of your personality and history. Just don't go overboard. Keep it concise. Remember, your goal is to give more of a sense of who you are and of your personality than it is to tell them your life story. You also don't need to tell them a detailed origin story of how you decided to write the book, why you started writing, or how much you love writing. It doesn't really matter to them.

And one additional word of advice for all previously published authors: it's so important to recognize that your previously published book probably isn't going to be what sells an agent on your new book, especially if it wasn't a wildfire bestseller. Instead, what's going to sell them on your new book is ... well, your new book. Make sure the query is primarily focused on your new project.

COMP TITLES CAN ADD FLAVOR

Unless the agent specifically asks for comp titles, adding them to a query letter is a strictly optional activity. But it can be helpful! Good comp titles can be a useful shorthand to give an agent the flavor of your book.

You can present your comp titles using a "[blank] meets [blank]" formulation or just say something along the lines of "My book would appeal to readers of [comp titles or comp authors]."

The key here is that an agent is going to be thinking about how your book can be positioned in the current landscape, which is why I think it's fine to use film and TV shows as comps in a query letter. The mood you want to strike them with is, "Oh yeah, I can see how there's a readership for this book." I'd recommend that at least one of the comp titles be relatively recently published or produced (within the last five years or so).

It's also important to strike a fine balance between mentioning books that are popular but not *too* popular. If the comp title is too popular, it doesn't help the agent hone in on the market since mega bestsellers pretty much appeal to everyone. (Also, trust me, the agent has heard books being compared to [insert mega bestseller] a million times before.) As a general rule of thumb, it's fine to mention bestsellers, but avoid books that are household names or veritable industries.

QUERY LETTER TIPS

- Try to keep your query letter between 250 and 350 words, including your bio and any personalization.
- Always specify your genre as well as your word count (novels) or anticipated word count (nonfiction).
- Keep the focus on the project you are querying about, even if you're a previously published author.
- It's important to convey flexibility with your ideas for sequels. As I spell out in more detail in

Rule #23, it's not a series until the second book is published. Your first novel needs to stand alone. Stick to something like this: *THE TITLE OF MY NOVEL is a [WORD COUNT] work of [GENRE]. It stands alone but I have ideas for expanding it into a series.*

- Always include a sample of your work (five pages are a good rule of thumb), even if the agent doesn't ask for it. No one is going to reject you for this, so this is the one place where I think it's permissible to break with submission guidelines. If you are e-mailing your query, be sure and paste this in the body of an e-mail. No attachments.

- Avoid gimmicks. Your protagonist shouldn't "write" your query letter, and there's no real need to think too far outside the box. Just write a good, solid query letter.

- YOU should write the query. Don't hire someone to write it for you. It's totally fine to get help editing it, but the essence should come from you.

- If you're e-mailing the query, be sure and include the word "Query" in the subject line. Sometimes emails land in spam filters, and this will help the agent fish it out. It's like your query's life raft!

- Within the publishing industry, book titles are typically written IN ALL CAPS. You're also fine italicizing titles if you want to, as no one is going to care that much. But don't capitalize character names in your query, as that's a movie business thing. Book agents don't need to be shouted at that DAN is dating CAROL.

HOW TO FORMAT YOUR QUERY LETTER

Don't. Get. Crazy.

Use block formatting. Double-space between paragraphs. Use a default font in a default size. Left justify.

The amount of time you spend formatting, coloring, bolding, italicizing, and adding pictures to your query is inversely proportional to how professional it looks when you're finished.

Rule #13
USE THIS QUERY LETTER TEMPLATE

You know those "mad lib" games you'd play as a kid, where you'd start off by writing down a list of verbs, places, and adjectives, and inevitably the words "snot" and "farted" were involved, which made any story HILARIOUS?

Well, we're going to play query letter mad lib today, which will give you a basic query letter template for fiction and narrative nonfiction. Keep on reading for other nonfiction, as I have tips for adapting this formula at the end of the chapter.

THE MAD LIB

Here's how it works. First, I'm going to need these things:

- Agent name
- Genre

- Personalized tidbit about agent
- Title of your book
- Word count
- Protagonist name
- Description of protagonist
- Setting
- Complicating incident (basically the big thing that happens in the beginning that sets your character on their way)
- Villain (doesn't have to be an actual person, alien, monkey, spore, etc. It could be a personality trait, nature, society ... basically whatever is standing between the protagonist and his/her/their/its goal)
- Verb that describes what your protagonist does to your villain
- Protagonist's quest
- Protagonist's goal
- Your publishing credits (optional)**
- Your name

Now, look how your query turns out:

Dear [Agent name],

I chose to submit to you because of your wonderful taste in [genre] and because you [personalized tidbit about agent].

[protagonist name] is a [description of protagonist] living in [setting]. But when [complicating incident], [protagonist name] must [protagonist's quest] and [verb] [villain] in order to [protagonist's goal].

[title] is a [word count] work of [genre]. I am the author of [author's credits (optional)], and this is my debut.

Thank you for your time, and I look forward to hearing from you soon.

Best wishes,
[your name]

That's all you need.

Now, granted, this is the most formulaic query ever written (you know ... because it uses a formula). Its purpose it to give you a starting place to then add personality by expanding with some flavor and detail. But if you can't fill this mad lib out in two seconds and craft a pretty decent query letter, something might be wrong with your book. These are the ingredients that absolutely positively completely totally must be in your query—if they are not, you have a problem. By all means, use your creativity, add some more description, embellish, and be an author (well, within reason).

But, it really doesn't need to be much more complicated than this.

THE FORMULA FOR NONFICTION

If you're writing non-narrative nonfiction, like self-help or business, the example above is still a decent template to follow, but rather than protagonists and villains, think in terms of the starting place, the challenges your target audience is facing, and the solutions you're offering.

Much like the template for fiction, in the query you're essentially starting with stasis (e.g., "X million people in America struggle with their weight"), the potential solution/complication that you're tackling ("What if they could all live flawlessly and effortlessly like [insert region with stereotypically beautiful people]?"), and the flavor of your book and your credentials and how you'll deliver on this promise ("I should know, I'm from [region], my abs melt steel, and I have more Instagram followers than all the Kardashians combined!").

Whatever you do, for nonfiction you must find a way to weave in your platform.

Rule #14
LEARN FROM OTHER SUCCESSFUL QUERIES

When it was time for me to find a literary agent for *Jacob Wonderbar and the Cosmic Space Kapow*, I used my own mad lib formula, personalized my query, and kept it under 300 words. And it worked! I practice what I preach, people.

Here's the query I sent:

Dear Ms. Drayton,

As a young literary agent with Curtis Brown Ltd. I have long admired Inkwell, as well as your strong track record. To paraphrase Douglas Adams, if

99

you searched for a book that was almost, but not quite, entirely unlike THE BOOK THIEF (which I absolutely loved), you might just have JACOB WONDERBAR AND THE COSMIC SPACE KAPOW, a middle-grade-and-up science fiction novel that I just completed. Still fun! But no one dies - Mr. Death would be lonely.

Jacob Wonderbar has been the bane of every substitute teacher at Magellan Middle School ever since his dad moved away from home. He never would have survived without his best friend Dexter, even if he is a little timid, and his cute-but-tough friend Sarah Daisy, who is chronically overscheduled. But when the trio meets a mysterious man in silver one night they trade a corn dog for his sassy spaceship and blast off into the great unknown. That is, until they break the universe in a giant space kapow and a nefarious space buccaneer named Mick Cracken maroons Jacob and Dexter on a tiny planet that smells like burp breath. The friends have to work together to make it back to their little street where the houses look the same, even as Earth seems farther and farther away.

JACOB WONDERBAR AND THE COSMIC SPACE KAPOW is 50,000 words and stands alone, but I have ideas for a series, including titles such as JACOB WONDERBAR FOR PRESIDENT OF THE UNIVERSE and JACOB WONDERBAR AND THE VACATIONING ALIENS FROM ANOTHER PLANET. I'm the author of an eponymous agenting and writing blog.

I'd be thrilled if you would consider WONDERBAR for representation, and a few other agents are considering simultaneously. Thanks very much, and hope to talk to you soon.

Nathan Bransford

Catherine Drayton at InkWell ended up offering me representation, and my trilogy was published by Dial Books at Penguin.

Want another example of a great query? Because I have another one!

Not only is my former client Lisa Brackmann's debut novel *Rock Paper Tiger* to die for, but when she originally contacted me she wrote one of the best queries I've ever received.

Without further ado:

Dear Mr. Bransford,

The Beijing '08 Olympics are over, the war in Iraq is lost, and former National Guard medic Ellie McEnroe is stuck in China, trying to lose herself in the alien worlds of performance artists and online gamers. When a chance encounter with a Chinese Muslim dissident drops her down a rabbit hole of conspiracies, Ellie must decide who to trust among the artists, dealers, collectors and operatives claiming to be on her side – in particular, a mysterious organization operating within a popular online game.

ROCK PAPER TIGER is a fast-paced, 108,000-word mainstream novel set in a China where the ultra-modern and cutting-edge clash with ancient neighborhoods and traditions, and in an America where the consequences of war reverberate long after the troops have come home. It will appeal to fans of William Gibson's books with contemporary settings, Laura Lippman's strong female protagonists, and almost anybody's whacked-out travelogues about the world's more surreal places.

I have a background in politics, Chinese history and the entertainment industry. I am working on a pop biography of Zhou Enlai for a small press and with a partner wrote a feature screenplay based on a series of Taiwanese fantasy novels, THE IMMORTALS, which was optioned by ActionGate Films. I was also a contributing editor for TWILIGHT OF EMPIRE: RESPONSES TO OCCUPATION, a collection of essays about the American occupation of Iraq (Perceval Press, 2004). I lived in China, travel there often and speak decent, if not quite fluent, Mandarin.

I'm querying you because you like novels set in foreign countries. Also, I hate the Lakers.

Best regards,
Lisa

This query is just stellar. It's well-written, it has a nice balance between key details (alien worlds of performance artists and gamers), plot (chance encounter drops her into a rabbit hole of conspiracies), personalization (knows my taste), and most importantly of all, she hates the Lakers. I had to restrain myself from immediately offering representation. I waited on the novel, which was amazing.

Rock Paper Tiger ended up being published by Soho Press, was named one of Amazon's best books of the year, and Lisa has gone on to have a very successful career as a novelist.

For nonfiction, it's crucial that the substance and key selling points of your book project come through in a clear way and that you offer sufficient information about your platform to convince the agent you're the right person to write the book.

Here's a great nonfiction query letter from author Michael Schreiber, which landed him literary agent Mitchell Waters:

Dear Mitchell,

We met last Monday evening at the Lammys. Imagine my delighted surprise when the category you got up to present – "best gay memoir/biography" – was the one in which my book, One-Man Show: The Life and Art of Bernard Perlin, was a finalist! Alas, One-Man Show lost out to Cleve Jones's When We Rise, but I'm nevertheless thrilled and proud to have been included in such extraordinary company, and to have been so honored for my very first book.

The reason I'm writing is that I am currently working on an authorized biography of the legendary Hollywood portrait artist Don Bachardy (http://www.donbachardy.com/index.php). This new book will explore Don Bachardy's storied life, illustrious friends and lovers (including his 30-year relationship with Christopher Isherwood), and astounding adventures through no-holds-barred interviews with the artist, never-before-seen photos, and an extensive selection of Don's incredible public and private art.

About me: I'm a teacher and writer based in Chicago. One-Man Show: The Life and Art of Bernard Perlin is my first book. In addition to its standing as a Lambda Literary Award Finalist, One-Man Show has also been named a 2017 Stonewall Honor Book by the American Library Association (the award will be presented at the end of this month) and finalist for the Eric Hoffer Book Award. The book is currently being adapted into a feature-length documentary film which will further explore Bernard Perlin's extraordinary, fearlessly lived life as a World War II correspondent, "magic realist" painter, sexual renegade, and gay artist.

I have also written for such publications as A&U: America's AIDS Magazine, The Archive: The Journal of the Leslie-Lohman Museum of Gay and Lesbian Art, The Gay & Lesbian Review, and Modern Magazine. For Bruno Gmünder, the publisher of One-Man Show, I am writing the introduction to a new book about the artist Bruce Sargeant. In addition, my husband Jason Loper and I are the creators of the popular blog This American House, which chronicles our adventures restoring our Frank Lloyd Wright-designed home in Iowa.

I'd be more than happy to send you a PDF or hard copy of One-Man Show and a selection of my interviews with Don Bachardy, if you might be interested. I thank you for giving this project your consideration, and look forward to communicating with you further. It was truly a pleasure to meet you at the Lammys!

Best regards,
Michael

Here's why I think this query letter works: the personalization is strong, the description of the nonfiction book project is clear, and the promise of what the book will offer is woven clearly into the summary. Michael clearly and succinctly documents the highlights of his platform and shows why he's not only the right person to write the book he's querying about but also why he would be a good client for the long haul.

Rule #15

SUMMARIZE THROUGH SPECIFICITY

Since "retiring" from being a literary agent, I've devoted much more time to freelance editing and working with authors on their queries (need personalized help? Feel free to reach out: nathan@nathanbransford.com).

This means that instead of just evaluating queries for a "yes" or "no," like I did when I was a literary agent, I've had to really get into the weeds to figure out *why* something works or doesn't work in order to deliver helpful feedback. It's given me a fresh look at what makes some queries sing, while others make a sad trombone noise.

I think I found the key: **summarizing through specificity.**

Writing a query is such a tricky balance. On the one hand, you have to condense an entire book into a few dozen words. On the other hand, you want your query to reflect the uniqueness of your book and stand out from the pack.

You need to be general, but you also need to include detail. You need to be clear, but you need to be original. You need to give flavor, but you can't get bogged down.

How in the world do you do all this at once?

Oh. I already told you. Summarizing through specificity.

Here's how to put this into practice in two simple steps.

LOOK FOR PLACES IN YOUR QUERY LETTER WHERE YOU DESCRIBE SOMETHING IN A GENERAL WAY

Oftentimes in queries you end up describing events in a very "summarizey" or generic way:

- Suzy "has to learn to grow up."
- The demon "haunts Bernadette's dreams."
- The wizard "must hone his magical powers."
- Boris "is a troublemaker."

While these phrases aren't terrible on their own, when you have too many of them the query ends up feeling flat. It misses the personality and flavor that makes your book awesome in the first place.

Instead ...

TRY TO REPLACE THIS GENERALITY WITH HOW IT ACTUALLY HAPPENS IN THE BOOK

Find the vague descriptions and replace them with specificity.

Let's try those plot summaries again:

- It's time for Suzy to trade her bottle of vodka for a can of corporate whupass.
- The demon waits for Bernadette to have a nightmare so that he can finally sink his claws into her.
- The wizard must figure out how to throw fireballs without burning down his hut again.
- Let's just say Boris was the best man at his bail bondsman's wedding.

Would you rather read the books described in Section 2 or Section 1? Nothing changed in the actual plots; what changed is that we replaced a broad, generic summary with some flavor-enhancing specificity.

Now, you may worry that if you get overly specific your query will get swamped in details without the bigger plot shining through. You'd be partly right. You can't do this trick endlessly, and you need to strike a balance. If you noticed, in my query letter for Jacob Wonderbar in Rule #14, I mixed up some generalities with specificity and tried to add little details that gives flavor to this world.

AVOID CLICHÉS AND DEAD PHRASES

Agents see phrases like these over and over and over and over again:

- "(something) ensued"
- "Literally."
- "in the worst way"
- "to the bitter end"
- "more than they bargained for"
- "has issues"
- "trials and tribulations"
- "comes of age"
- "an incredible journey"
- "he must (something) and (something) before (important object) falls into the wrong hands"

Not only are they clichés, they're hopelessly vague. They don't really tell us more about what is actually happening in the story.

Go through your query with a fine-toothed cliché comb ($14.99 while supplies last) and get all these vague turns of phrases out of there. Replace them with specificity and your query will sing.

Rule #16
WRITE A SYNOPSIS

Of all the things that novelists will write through-out the traditional publishing process, a synopsis may be what's dreaded the most. Not every agent or editor will ask you for a synopsis, but chances are you're going to have to write one at some point. So, rather than scrambling when you're asked for one later, you might as well tackle it at the start.

It's not fun to cram an entire novel into a relatively brief summary, and these tend to be even harder to write than the dastardly query letter, but if you follow just a few relatively simple steps and keep a few key things in mind, it may still be a pain, but it won't be endlessly hard.

First, though, what is a synopsis?

It is essentially **a summary of what actually happens in a book.** That's it. It's a summary of the book that includes the ending. Agents typically ask for them when they request your manuscript during the querying stage in order to get a sense of the entirety of the book. It also gives them something to refer to when they later need to refresh their memory on character names, plot points, or other key details, and it may be a part of what they submit to editors. You may later need to write brief synopses for future installments of a multi-book deal to give an editor a sense of where you want to take a series.

A synopsis is slightly different from a query letter, which includes biographical information, and it's also different than jacket copy, which is oriented to selling a book to a reader and thus avoids spoilers. You have room to include greater detail, but the synopsis should still cover the arc of the book in a relatively succinct way.

Unlike the way manuscripts are formatted, synopses are typically single-spaced and are typically two to four pages long.

Here are some key elements that set snappy synopses apart from dreary ones.

SUMMARIZE THROUGH SPECIFICITY

Just as in a query, the more detail you can infuse into the synopsis, the more it will come to life. Ditch all discussion of themes and what the novel means and focus on what happens. Some summarizing will be necessary, but those little moments where you show what makes your character and world unique will make the synopsis sparkle.

Also, focus on using precise descriptions to make sure the stakes are clear. What happens if the protagonist succeeds? What if they fail? Infuse the synopsis with this knowledge so the reader knows why they should care.

USE A COHESIVE VOICE

If you have a novel that alternates between several different characters or has a unique structure, it may be difficult to figure out how to describe the plot in a clear way. You don't want to write a synopsis that constantly alternates between different plot-lines and characters or you're going to bewilder the reader.

Instead, don't be beholden to the precise sequence in which events unfold in your novel or to an alternating-character structure, and try as much as possible to "get above it" and focus on describing the essential events in a way that's clear to the reader.

This could mean sticking to one character per paragraph, it could mean describing the plot from an omniscient perspective, and it will almost always mean describing your novel in third person even if your novel is written in first person. Whatever you do, optimize for clarity and cohesion in describing the plot over being a stickler for how things unfold linearly in the novel.

Don't worry about spoilers! Agents and editors read so many books and are so well-acquainted with the sausage-making of writing that they probably aren't going to be surprised by even the most supposedly surprising endings. Surprises are for mortal readers. Agents can see them coming a mile away. They're even experienced enough to do the mental jujitsu of judging whether an ending will be surprising to someone who has never read the book *even though the agent/editor knows exactly how it ends*. They can put themselves in another reader's shoes and judge it that way.

It's unlikely that your book is going to be made or broken by how well you write a synopsis, and it's not something that will likely see the light of day beyond your agent and editor. Don't overrate its importance. Instead, have fun with your synopsis, and use it as valuable practice for summarizing your book in a most awesome way.

Rule #17
SEND YOUR QUERY LETTER OUT IN BATCHES

Once you've written a fantastic query letter and compiled a list of reputable literary agents who specialize in your genre, it's go time, baby.

(Note: the strategy in this chapter also applies if you are choosing to go directly to publishers or hybrid publishers.)

Let's talk for a second about what not to do when sending out a query letter.

One of the more mystifying ways that some aspiring authors go about the query process is to blast an e-mail to every single agent in the publishing industry with a "To My Future Literary Agent" subject line.

When I was an agent, what made me slap my head wasn't just that it's poor e-mail etiquette or knowing that 1,000 of my closest colleagues were also considering the project at exactly the same time. It's just not a good strategy.

What if you didn't get the pitch right and everyone rejects (or ignores) you all at once? Well, you blew your chance to tweak it a bit and try again with another round. (And no, you can't just tweak it and re-send it to those 1,000 agents again, as that's a good way to get blocked forever.)

If you rush the submission process, you lose the ability to evaluate and adjust as you go.

It's much smarter and more effective to send out the query in batches of 7–10 at a time. When you get a rejection, send a new one out. If a few months go by and you haven't heard from an agent, consider it a rejection and send a new one out.

Take your time. See what the response is like. If you're not getting any requests, you can take another hard look at your query and opening and think about making adjustments. As time goes by, you might notice something you could do better or receive a valuable piece of feedback. If, on the other hand, you're getting manuscript requests but not an offer, you will know you're at least on the right track but maybe just haven't found the right fit.

Going at a steady pace can be frustrating and feel tedious sometimes, but it gives you time to look at your query and opening with fresh eyes as your results come in.

Also, take note: in this day and age, sending out a query letter is not the only way to approach agents! There are pitch wars, hashtags on Twitter, and you can meet literary agents at conferences.

I would still resist the temptation of jumping the gun and pitching via other channels to test the waters before you're ready to pair it with a traditional query letter strategy. Many experienced agents still only accept traditional query letters, and you might miss out on a potential opportunity if you get caught up in the rush and limit yourself to only one channel.

After you've sent your query letter off into the great unknown, you sit back and wait for the literary agent to consider it. And wait. And wait some more.

Here's what's happening on an agent's end: First, they print out all the queries and stack them up. Then, they spread them around the room until they're a few inches deep. Next, they lie down, wave their arms and legs, and make query angels.

Actually, it works like this. An agent will weigh the quality of your query, the marketability of your book idea, and your platform/qualifications, and then they will combine it with a dash of their personal taste and gut feeling and decide whether they want to request a proposal (nonfiction) or a partial or full manuscript (fiction).

If you get requests, your query letter has done its job, and you have moved on to the next step!

Bear in mind that many/most literary agents have a no-response-means-no policy, so if you do not hear back after a couple of months, you have your answer. As we covered in Rule #8, it is not customary to follow-up if you haven't heard back on a query letter.

Keep your cool, stay calm, and be professional throughout the process. Patience in the submission process (and life, for that matter) goes a long way.

Rule #18
SHOW PERSONALITY

At some point during your agent hunt, an agent may offer to work with you on a revision without offering representation. This can create enough thorny situations that it's worth tackling in a standalone rule.

For instance, your manuscript may already be out with other agents, and you may be unsure whether to put things on hold to work on a revision or wait and see if other agents like the project as it is. An agent may also be asking you to put in work to revise your proposal or manuscript with no guarantee it's going to result in them taking you on as a client.

What are you to do?

First, it's helpful to break these situations into categories to wrap your head around what happens in each scenario.

SCENARIO 1: AN AGENT SUGGESTS SOME FEEDBACK, FOLLOWED BY AN INVITATION TO RESUBMIT AFTER A REVISION.

The good news: It's not a no!!

In this scenario, unless specified otherwise, the agent will probably assume that you're going to continue querying or talking to other agents, but if you decide to revise, they'll take another look.

When I was an agent, I would sometimes do this when there were fixable problems, such as writerly tics that distracted me from the narrative or a particular character that wasn't working. Or when the project had some promise but just wasn't quite there.

When it's relatively general feedback and an agent isn't sending a big, long editorial letter, usually they won't offer representation at this stage and it's more of an invitation to keep communication lines open.

SCENARIO 2: AN AGENT WANTS TO WORK WITH YOU ON A DEEP EDIT

In this case, the agent wants to provide copious, extensive notes in the hopes that with a revision (or two or three or four) the manuscript will be in a place where they'll be able to submit the project to editors.

In this scenario, whether you've explicitly discussed exclusivity or not, if the agent is investing this much time in your project, they are likely assuming that you are going to give them first crack at representing the revised project. If you were to take the manuscript you improved with one agent and let another agent represent it, the revising agent would likely be hexing you and using your book jacket as a dart board on publication day.

Within Scenario 2 there are *two more* customary scenarios that involve exclusivity and representation. Agentception!

- **Agent offers representation before embarking upon revision.** Some agents want to snap up a possibly hot project and will take on the client before they embark upon revisions. (See Rule #19 on how to handle an offer of representation.) The author is happy (they have an agent!), and the agent knows the author won't ditch them for another agent once the manuscript is completed without having to formally cancel a legal document. The downside with this scenario is that embarking on revisions is a murky, tricky, stressful process. Who knows where the revision will lead and if both author and agent will be ready for it to be sent out when it's complete? Who knows if the agent and author will work well together? Which is why, when I was a literary agent, I tended to prefer ...

- **Agent signs up author *after* the revision is completed if both author and agent**

are happy. Some agents want to see how the relationship works during the revision, and they want to make sure that they are totally enthusiastic about the revised manuscript/proposal before they formally commit to the author. On the plus side for the author, there is no official commitment in place, other than an informal agreement on exclusivity while they're working on the edits. If, after completing the revision, in good faith the author doesn't feel that the author/agent relationship is working or isn't happy about the direction of the manuscript, they too can walk away. (After having a conversation with the agent; please don't just take the revision and ghost.) It takes some faith and trust on both sides to proceed in this manner, but I took on several clients this way and felt like it ended up being very fair for both sides.

Ultimately, as the author, you have to decide whether the edits are resonating with you, whether you want to make the changes, and whether you are feeling good about working with the agent. If you are, great! Keep moving forward! If you're not, trust your gut!

But, uh, while you're editing your project, what do you do about all those other agents that you've been querying in the meantime?

HOW TO KEEP OTHER AGENTS APPRISED OF A REVISION

There are few cut and dry situations here, and navigating these edits may require some judgment calls on your part.

Let's start with the clear-cut scenarios:

- **An agent offers you representation before you embark on an edit:** Follow the procedure laid out in Rule #19.
- **An agent asks that you work together exclusively on an edit:** You need to be able to grant the agent this exclusivity. If other agents have your manuscript, give them a heads-up that an agent has requested that you work together exclusively on an edit, and request that they get back to you within 7–14 days on whether they'd like to offer representation. After this time period, you'll either have an offer or you'll be free to proceed with the edit.

Often, though, it won't be this clear cut. An agent will just provide some feedback and invite you to re-submit, and you'll have to decide whether to make the edits, and then, once you've made the edits, whether you want to send the new manuscript/proposal to any other agents who were currently considering the old one.

Tread very, very carefully here. It's such a tricky situation. On the one hand, you want the agents to be considering the best manuscript/proposal possible, and the edits the previous agent provided might well have improved the project. On the other hand, agents can get royally annoyed if they spend hours reading a manuscript only to get pinged by the author with a new version, essentially forcing them to start over.

Here is the main factor to weigh: **How substantive are the changes?**

If the changes are major and fundamentally alter the project, I would take the risk and swap in the new version, apologizing to the agent profusely for the inconvenience. If the changes are more cosmetic, even if they improve the project on the whole, I would probably sit tight. (Also, this goes for any changes to your project, including revisions that you undertook yourself. Don't swap in a new manuscript unless you absolutely have to.)

Be honest with yourself about this. I know it's tricky to suss out the line between substantive and cosmetic, but I would err on the side of not bothering the other agents. They might have a totally different reaction to your work than the first agent, and chances are the essence of your project is still coming through.

Rule #19
HANDLE AN OFFER OF REPRESENTATION LIKE A PRO

The day an agent offers you representation is one of the most incredible moments in your publishing journey. I'll never forget the moment when Catherine Drayton called me to offer representation for *Jacob Wonderbar*. I had doubted myself nearly every step of the way before that point and hadn't even told my friends and family I was working on a novel.

Suddenly, there was someone else who believed in my book's potential! A publishing professional, no less!

Because of this inevitable rush of euphoria, it's all the more important to plan out your strategy for handling this offer ahead of time. Don't immediately yell, "YES, DEAR LORD, YES!" even if you really, really want to. Take your time to make sure it's the right fit.

This is a crucial conversation. It bears repeating: a bad agent (or a bad relationship with your agent) can do more harm to your writing career than having no agent. If an agent sends out your work to publishers, that's your shot. You don't get a second one with the same project. Be absolutely sure it's a good fit.

Having been on both sides of this phone call, as both an agent and an author, here's my advice for how to handle an offer of representation.

THANK THE AGENT AND SET UP A DIFFERENT TIME TO TALK

Even if your agent calls to give you the good news, sure, have a conversation with them, thank them for believing in you, but schedule another time to talk through the logistics.

You'll probably need some time to mentally prep for the conversation, as well as to handle any necessary follow-ups with other agents who have your manuscript (more on that in a sec). Give the prospective agent a time-frame for the conversation that accounts for these follow-ups.

Don't worry about putting off the full conversation, as you're not going to offend the agent. They expect that you'll take some time to think it through and make sure it's a good fit. (If they're putting pressure on you to decide, don't necessarily run away, but be wary).

Also, don't worry about the agent thinking you're weird for being a blubbering, excited mess. They've seen it all (and they're excited, too).

FOLLOW UP WITH THE OTHER AGENTS WHO HAVE YOUR WORK

If other agents have already requested your manuscript, it's customary to give them a heads-up that you have received an offer of representation and to give them a reasonable time frame (7–14 days) to consider your work.

Opinions vary a bit on whether to follow up with agents who only have your query and haven't requested your manuscript. I don't personally advise this, but some agents do expect it, and if you have a dream agent on this list, it wouldn't hurt to let him or her know.

Regardless of what you decide on this, I wouldn't advise taking the offer from the agent and then blasting out a million new queries to everyone else on your list. That's not cool. Be respectful to the agents who jumped first.

Also, even if the agent making you an offer is at the very top of your wish list, it may still be helpful to follow through with some outreach to the other agents who may be reading your work. You'll benefit from the additional conversations even if you go with the original agent, and you'll be more confident in your choice.

TRIPLE-CHECK ONCE MORE THAT THE AGENT IS REPUTABLE

You should have already done this step when you researched your list of literary agents after reading Rule #11, but it doesn't hurt to check again.

PREP YOUR LIST OF QUESTIONS

Now it's time to get ready for the follow-up call in which you and your future agent will discuss your work together in more detail. It will help to come prepared to this conversation. It's okay if you have a million questions. Here are the ones I think are especially important:

- **What do they like about your book?** This is such a simple but crucial question. Hopefully the agent already communicated this when they offered you representation, but if they didn't, ask. Why? 1) If they're faking their enthusiasm, you'll know it (and if they're a scammer or bad agent, they'll probably stumble through it). 2) Their answer will help you make sure they get both you and your book.

- **What is their communication style?** This one is super important. Agents vary greatly in their approach to the information they communicate to their clients and how often they communicate it. Some agents share everything, including all rejection letters, while some check in at periodic intervals and just share a summary. Some agents get back to you in 24 hours, while some take a month or two. Some give their clients discretion over what they see. Try to suss out their style and make sure it works for you.

- **Is there an author/agency agreement?** Most agents (though not all) have author/agency agreements that you'll need to sign in order to become a client. Make sure that you understand and are comfortable with everything in the author/agency agreement and that there's a reasonable termination clause if things don't work out. Note that most agents will have the right to receive commission for deals when they have submitted on your behalf, even if you then part ways (so you can't get a deal and then just bounce on them to avoid the commission). PLEASE NOTE: I'm not an attorney, so don't construe this as legal advice. Consult a publishing attorney if you have any questions.

- **What's the normal time-frame for remitting advances and royalty payments?**

The author/agency agreement (as well as your eventual agreement with a publisher) will likely have a provision that will direct the publisher to pay the agency, which will then subtract your commission and pay you the balance. Find out how long this turnaround usually takes.

- **What incidental charges will you be responsible for?** As you should know by now, but once more for the people in the back, agents shouldn't charge you anything up front (they get paid when you get paid). The exception is that they may recoup incidental charges, like copying and things like this. Make sure you know what these charges are and that you're comfortable with them.

- **Is he or she interested in you for just this book or for others as well?** This isn't necessarily the time to pitch the agent on the seventeen manuscripts in your drawer, but you should understand whether the agent is interested in more projects from you no matter what happens with this particular book. They may want to focus on this first one and see what happens, but find out how and when they want to discuss future book projects.

- **Do they plan to only submit to the major publishers or will they submit until the bitter end?** That last part is a little hyperbolic, but this is really important. Bear in mind that an agent receives a 15% commission on any advance, and small presses may well only offer in the low $1,000s of dollars. Multiply $1,500 x 15%, calculate the hours involved in submitting a project for the agent, and you'll see they would be lucky to crack minimum wage. Some agents are still willing to go to small presses in the hopes of building up an author over the long haul, but others may want to stop at the majors. Make sure you're satisfied with the agent's plan and approach.

- **How does the agency handle subsidiary rights, like audio and film?** Some agents have in-house departments to handle film rights, while some will work with other outside agents. Make sure you understand how it works.

- **Does the manuscript need any changes or are you good to go?** Some agents are hands-on and will work with an author on revisions, while others only take on projects they think are ready to go. Don't be alarmed by either answer, but if the agent does want changes, make sure they're consistent with your vision for the book.

- **Can you talk to some of their other clients?** Bear in mind that, almost by definition, these authors are going to be happy with their agent. So, don't look to these conversations to help you with an overall verdict, but do try to suss out or double-check some of the things that are important to you, like communication style.

- **Anything else that is important to you.** Seriously. Now's the time.

GO WITH YOUR GUT

Try to be as calm as possible for this conversation, be honest and transparent with everyone throughout the process, and listen to what the agent (or agents) has to say, and the answer will become clear.

And then you'll have an advocate who believes in your work. Huzzah!

Rule #20
ESTABLISH TRUST AND COMMUNICATE WITH YOUR AGENT

Every author/agent relationship is different, but they all depend on two essential ingredients: **trust** and **communication**.

Over the course of your relationship with your agent, you are going to go through some great times and some not so great times. You're going to have to deliver difficult truths to each other. You're going to have to trust that your agent has your best interests at heart and is working hard on your behalf, and they will have to trust that *you* will fulfill your responsibilities and not go rogue.

Trust your agent. I really can't emphasize enough how important this is. Some authors I've spoken to are incredibly paranoid that their agent is going to pull one over on them and are looking for a scam around every corner.

Trust that there is very little incentive for a reputable agent to scam their clients, and while scandals do happen from time to time (as in any industry), they're mercifully uncommon. Agents rely heavily on their reputations in this business, and their financial incentives are aligned with yours. They want you to succeed as much as you want to succeed.

By all means, make sure you understand what's happening, but there's no reason to go into this process with your hackles raised.

The essential second element is **communication**. The lines of dialogue must be open. I can't even begin to count the number of authors who email me with very simple questions just because they're scared to ask their agent.

Your agent is not a delicate flower that only blooms once a year and disappears into the ground if you whisper in its direction. If you are uncomfortable, talk to your agent. If you are unhappy, talk to your agent. If you have some serious concerns, talk to your agent. Give your agent a chance to address problems. They can't do this if you're not communicating with them.

All that said, trust your gut. Problems can arise. Agents can be notoriously uncommunicative. You may not have a clear picture of what's really going on. So, yes. Try first to live according to the principles of trust and communication, but there are situations when challenges arise that may be impossible to overcome.

Leaving an agent is a really tough decision, and it shouldn't be taken lightly. You are forgoing an advocate, and could possibly be burning a bridge, so it's incredibly important to act as carefully and rationally as possible.

But, sometimes leaving your agent is the right decision. An ineffective author/agent relationship can be seriously damaging, and I've seen many careers take off when an author transitioned from a bad agent to a good agent, or from a bad fit with an otherwise-good agent to a good fit with an also-good agent.

It's not always easy to know when to leave, which is why it's important to try to suss out whether your concerns are valid or whether you're letting your emotions get the best of you.

Even the best agents strike out sometimes, and not every book sells. This doesn't make them a bad agent. Sometimes, it just doesn't happen with the first book. If they made a good faith effort to submit it, they did the best they could but struck out with editors, and they still believe in you, this alone is not a very good reason to leave.

But if you find that your agent is being shady or doing something head-slappingly bad, like blasting your manuscript to 50 editors all at once on the same email thread, have a heart to heart. If they don't have an explanation that satisfies you or you can't get in touch with them despite repeated attempts, you may have your answer.

Before you part ways, if you have concerns, express them. Give your agent one last shot to address them. They should appreciate your honesty and have good answers for you.

After this conversation, if your gut is telling you it's time to go, it's time to go. It's your career. You have to do what you think is best. If you have acted in good faith, listened, and you just think it's time, it may well be time.

Make sure you understand how termination works in your author/agency agreement and then go forth on your separate ways. But, do this *before* you try to seek new representation.

Rule #21
KNOW WHEN TO SUBMIT DIRECTLY TO PUBLISHERS

As you know from, well, pretty much everything I've said up until this point, if you are attempting to publish traditionally, it is advisable to try to find a literary agent to submit to publishers on your behalf. Many publishers, especially the major ones, won't accept unagented submissions.

And take heed: **if you send your manuscript out to a bunch of publishers without an agent, you could be harming your chances of finding a publisher down the line.** Most agents won't resubmit to a publisher who has already considered a project, even if it was sent to the publisher unagented and even if it subsequently undergoes a revision (unless the editor specifically asks to see a new version). And who knows, the publishers could have been interested if it had gone through the proper channels.

There are some exceptions where it's acceptable, even advantageous, to submit to publishers without a literary agent, and it's good to be familiar with them.

Here they are.

YOU MET AN EDITOR, MADE A PERSONAL CONNECTION, AND THEY OFFERED TO CONSIDER YOUR WORK

Via a writer's conference, publishing industry event, MFA program, or even social networks, you might end up meeting an editor who expresses an interest in your work.

So, sure! You have their attention. Send it to them.

Even if you do this, however, I would still try simultaneously to find a literary agent. Mention to the editor when you reach out that you're in the process of finding an agent so they're not caught off guard. Don't worry, an editor won't think this is weird (or at least, they shouldn't), and if they like your work, they might even end up helping you to land an agent.

YOUR BOOK FITS INTO A NICHE MARKET

There are a ton of independent and small presses out there that specialize in very specific markets, such as niche science books, regional history, or New Age. Since the advances and sales involved are usually small, it's often customary for authors and editors to simply work directly together because it's not viable for agents to take the time to represent authors for 15% of the amounts involved.

It would be tricky for me to break down all the genres and topics that could be considered "niche," but do the research to see what is customary for your genre/niche and research the publishers for books similar to yours.

YOU ALREADY TRIED QUERYING AGENTS, YOU CAME UP EMPTY, AND YOU WANT TO TRY WITH EDITORS DIRECTLY

Did you query every literary agent under the sun and come up short? What's the harm in sending it out to some editors?

Now, bear in mind that this is the longest of long shots, especially if you're going to try with one of the Big 5 publishers. As I said, most editors won't consider unagented projects, and you may end up in a dust bin.

But, I have seen it happen! Just remember, this should be a last resort, since an agent won't be likely to consider representing this project once you've already sent your work out.

HOW TO WORK DIRECTLY WITH PUBLISHERS

If you do end up going for it unagented, here are some recommendations:

- **Be transparent with an editor if you are simultaneously searching for representation.** Many editors would actually prefer to work with a literary agent because it streamlines the process and usually means less work for them. Others may not be so psyched because agents tend to get better deals for their clients and will be tougher negotiators. Err on the side of transparency.

- **If you get an offer, it's okay to use that offer to try to find an agent.** Sure, you did a lot of the hard work, but if you do get an offer without an agent, having an agent to negotiate the contract alone is worth 15%. Don't leave the editor endlessly hanging as you try to find an agent, though, and once again, be transparent.

- **If you do the deal directly, consult with a publishing attorney or someone who knows publishing contracts before you sign.** Even if you're a lawyer or have one handy, it's important to find someone who knows what's customary in the publishing industry rather than a general expert on contracts. You need to find someone who knows things like which rights and options are customary to grant to a publisher to help you make sure you're getting a good deal.

- **Do your research.** There are some fantastic small presses out there that can really give your book a leg up. There are others that may be well-intentioned but that aren't going to do more for you than you could do on your own via self-publishing. And then there are scam artists out there who will try to prey on your vanity and offer you a disadvantageous "book deal." Vet anyone you're working with very thoroughly.

There are lots of different paths to successful publication, so don't rule out this option, but be extra careful that you're taking the right steps for your book.

Rule #22
FAMILIARIZE YOURSELF WITH THE BASICS OF PUBLISHING CONTRACTS

As I mentioned in the last rule, before you sign a publishing contract you should either have a literary agent or consult with someone who knows what they're doing. It's crucial to find an expert who isn't just familiar with contracts generally but who understands what's customary in the book business so that they can effectively provide guidance on potential red flags.

Please don't construe this section as legal advice, as I'm not an attorney, but in order to help you understand what publishing deals entail, here are some typical sections of publishing contracts.

TERRITORY

The territory is a list of countries where a publisher can distribute. There are four basic types of deals for English language publishers:

- **US or North America**. This gives the publisher the exclusive right to sell/distribute the book in the English language in either just the US or the US and Canada. (Note that North America typically does not include Mexico and other Latin American countries.)
- **British Commonwealth**. In the UK, it's common for the publisher to have exclusive rights in not only the UK but also in many former colonies and some random islands that I had never even heard of before I worked in book publishing.
- **World English**. Just like it sounds. The publisher can sell/distribute/license the book in the English language throughout the world.
- **World All Languages**. Just like World English, only with all the world's lovely and colorful languages thrown in. The publisher can license the book to be translated into other languages and sold in all territories of the world.

As the internet opens up avenues for distribution, these exclusive territories and what's called "open market" rights to sell non-exclusively elsewhere are becoming more and more contentious, and publishers will often try to secure rights everywhere.

GRANT OF RIGHTS

These are the specific rights that are granted in the agreement. Sometimes this can mean everything under the sun (book rights, film rights, audio rights, tv rights, electronic rights, and even theme park rights), or it could just be for one specific thing (trade paperback reprint rights only).

There is also a term attached for how long those rights will be held. It could be for a specific length of time (such as 7 years) or it could be for the life of the copyright of the book.

Agents will try to hold onto as many rights as they possibly can because it's more profitable to do a deal directly with, say, a film studio rather than having to split the revenue with the publisher. Audio and film rights are two areas where agents will fight very hard to retain rights for the author. Publishers, of course, always try to get every right they can, even if they don't have immediate plans to exploit them.

ADVANCE

The advance is the money that a publisher pays you up front to publish the book. Take it to the bank, as it's yours to keep, even if your book only sells two copies. Huzzah!

As I outlined in Rule #2, think of an advance as a loan that you don't have to pay back. Each copy you sell earns royalties (discussed below) that first go toward paying off your advance. Then, if your book royalties eventually surpass your initial advance, you start to receive royalty payments.. So, if you were paid $10,000, your book has to earn $10,000 in royalties before you start to see any extra money.

Advances can range from a hundred dollars to BILLIONS. (Okay, not billions. Unless you're Dan Brown. Okay, not even Dan Brown.)

Advances are typically paid in installments tied to certain benchmarks along the way to publication, like the signing of the contract, delivery and acceptance of the manuscript, and publication. A good agent will try to negotiate these installments so that they're paid to the author as soon as possible.

ROYALTIES

Each copy you sell earns a royalty, specified as either a percentage of the cover price or a percentage of the amount a publisher receives for the sale. There are lots of different types of royalties depending on what type of copy is sold (hardcover, paperback, mass market, special sales, discount sales, omnibus, anthology ... it goes on and on).

SUBRIGHTS

In addition to printing and selling your book, publishers also typically get assorted rights that they may or may not sell to another publisher or publication somewhere down the line. It's sort of like subcontracting—if a publisher doesn't want to do something themselves, they can license the rights to someone else. The subrights section will specify the revenue splits if the publisher sells these subrights to another entity.

So, let's say a publisher publishes your book in hardcover. They can either bring out a paperback edition OR they can sell paperback rights to another publisher, in which case publisher #2 does all the work to bring out the paperback edition, and you and publisher #1 share the proceeds based on the split specified in the subrights section.

DELIVERY DATES

During the offer stage, all the dates should be worked out for delivery of the manuscript, and they will be specified here.

WARRANTY AND INDEMNITY

This sounds like a spy novel, but actually this is the part where you promise the publisher that your book isn't plagiarized, that you control all the rights, that any recipes are not injurious to the user, etc., etc. Basically, you promise on your life that everything in your book is kosher and accept responsibility for it.

This clause also specifies what happens if you and/ or the publisher are sued for any kind of infringement, whether real or frivolous. It hopefully won't come up, but make sure you understand what's outlined here, and this is yet another section where it's particularly helpful to have a review from someone with publishing expertise.

REVERSIONS

This is an important clause because it specifies when the publisher will return their rights to you if they're not actively selling your book or the sales drop below a certain threshold for a certain length of time. When this happens, the rights revert back to the author. Typically, the publisher has the opportunity to sell off their remaining stock of books, but then the contract terminates and the author is free to go off on their own.

The principle here is that you don't want a publisher just sitting on the rights to your book without actively selling it, preventing you from either finding another publisher or re-publishing it yourself.

This is another contract section that has become increasingly contentious as publishers can now count on a continuous trickle of sales via online distribution and print on demand and want to hold onto the rights as long as possible, but authors may want to be free to pursue their own avenues once a publisher isn't actively promoting it.

ACCOUNTING

This section (or sections) will specify when you will receive royalty statements that track book sales and when royalty payments will be made.

If the contract is for multiple books, it will also specify whether there is joint or separate accounting. Joint accounting means that the books need to earn out the entire advance with cumulative book sales, whereas with separate accounting each individual book is accounted separately.

Separate accounting tends to be more advantageous for authors since there's a lower threshold to earn out and one book might be a bigger hit than the other, increasing the odds of receiving additional royalties.

OPTIONS

Oftentimes a publisher will request a first look at your next work, and it will be specified in this section.

Be VERY VERY VERY careful with these options. Don't let a publisher tie up your rights with needless open-ended options. Unscrupulous publishers often try to lock an author down practically for life, which can be hugely damaging to your career.

There are many other sections to publishing contracts, and much of this may be sailing over your head, which is why I must reiterate that it's really crucial to either a) have an agent who knows what they're doing or b) consult with a publishing attorney or expert who knows what they're doing.

Know what you sign!

Rule #23
BE FLEXIBLE
ABOUT SEQUELS

Series are a tricky beast.

On the one hand, particularly in certain genres, a series can be a great way to build a fan base around popular characters and can give an author a chance to really flesh out a world. Series can be extremely successful.

On the other hand, it requires a bigger commitment from a publisher, it may pigeonhole an author for that all-important second book, and an agent or editor may want the author to tackle something new or branch off in a different direction. It all depends on the genre, the idea, the author, the publishing house, the agent, the editor, the weather, the astrological conditions, and, of course, which side of the bed the respective parties involved woke up on.

Ultimately, as I tell authors all the time, **it's not a series until the second book is published.**

When you have an idea for a series, be flexible. That first book should be able to stand by itself, whether or not it's eventually expanded into a series. This way, if your agent or eventual editor thinks it should be a stand-alone, that's cool. If they agree that it would make a killer series, that's cool, too.

Think of it as writing a novel that's more *Star Wars* than *Empire Strikes Back*. Sure, Darth Vader was flying away at the end of *Star Wars*, but that was a self-contained movie that didn't leave too many cliffs dangling. In *Empire Strikes Back,* on the other hand, Han Solo was left frozen in FREAKING CARBONITE, and I don't think audiences would have been satisfied had that been the end of the movie without a sequel in the works. If you write an *Empire Strikes Back* novel and your agent/editor wants it to be a stand-alone, well, they're not going to love the ending.

Thus, in queries I would suggest to the agent that the idea *could* be expanded into a series, but I wouldn't really convey that you're dead-set on it being a series. This way the door is open for both possibilities, and you're not putting yourself in a box. Or carbonite.

You can't go wrong with some variation of the following: *THE TITLE OF MY NOVEL is a [WORD COUNT] work of [GENRE]. It stands alone, but I have ideas for expanding it into a series.*

I can understand why people love writing series. Writers grow attached to the worlds they create, the characters become friends, and it becomes familiar, and they just keep on writing in these worlds because they love them. It feels amazing to flesh out a world in multiple novels. I've been there.

But, it's so important to be able to walk away for something new if the market demands it. You created one amazing world, so trust that you can create another!

Rule #24
BRACE YOURSELF FOR THE WAITING

When I first tried to find a literary agent for *Jacob Wonderbar*, I was actually a literary agent at the time. "So this will be a piece of cake," I thought.

I sent queries to all the agent friends I knew, and ... they all rejected me. All of them. I eventually ended up finding an agent who I didn't know personally.

Then, when my manuscript went out to publishers, I really thought I was going to be completely cool about the submission process. I was an agent! I'd seen this before! I'd sold projects that were out on submission for six months and even a year! How hard could it be?

Being a Big Bad Experienced Agent, how long did it take me to crack?

A week and a half.

A WEEK AND A HALF.

That's how long it took before I woke up in the middle of the night, checked my e-mail, crawled onto the floor, and whispered, "It's not going to sell! It's not going to sell. I can't believe it, it's not going to sell."

It sold. *Jacob Wonderbar* ended up going to an auction with multiple bids a few weeks later, and I ended up with Penguin as my publisher.

I knew better than to freak out, and I *still* freaked out! Even when books sell, they almost never sell in a week and a half. A book selling in a week and a half is almost unheard of. I knew that. But for some reason, everything I knew went straight out the window once I went on submission. It's like I turned into a phlebotomist who's afraid of needles.

Luckily, I was able to keep my panic within the walls of my apartment, but all the same: the experience gave me a huge amount of respect for just how hard it is to wait for news about your manuscript.

Writing is hard. It's time-consuming, it's solitary ... it's hard. But, at least it's within your control. You can change things, you can work harder and revise more, and it's all within your reach.

The frustrating thing about submitting to agents and editors is that there's nothing. you. can. do. about. it. Once you hit "send," you're at their mercy.

The stress of wondering, day after day, if today is the day you're going to receive good or bad news, always sneaking peeks at your e-mail, trying to be cool and composed, hearing "No" all those times before you get your "Yes" ... it's a steady stress that can quickly wear you down.

This is compounded by something I like to call Publishing Time.

As anyone even remotely connected with the book world knows, things take forever in publishing. The industry works according to its own speed, and it's a speed that people in other industries tend to find equal parts bewildering and maddening.

It can take ages for aspiring authors to hear back on their queries and manuscripts. It can take ages for an agent to hear back from editors about a book project, even on something like a short nonfiction proposal or a picture book manuscript. It takes forever for books to come out. It takes forever for checks to come from publishers (I shake my fist at you!!).

Now, let me first say that there is a fairly good, if incomplete, explanation for the pace of publishing. A lot of people have to read a book in order to get it from an unsolicited query to a bookstore. And reading takes time. Selling into bookstores and developing and executing marketing plans take lead time.

The industry is also populated by a lot of very creative people, and creative types aren't exactly known for their punctuality. (I will also say that there *are* plenty of very punctual people in publishing who work with incredible speed and dexterity, and I love them dearly.)

It's not fun to have to wait a long time for every seemingly interminable step of the publishing process. Try not to blame the professionals. Just keep at it.

And, no matter how many times you crawl onto the floor in agony, try as best you can to stay cool and enjoy the process.

Rule #25
BE A PRO ON THE WAY TO PUBLICATION

Remember all those stories about great cantankerous authors way back when who were legendarily inebriated most of the time, were notoriously difficult to handle, got into fisticuffs, and were generally misanthropic to every human they encountered, but people still published their books because they were wonderfully talented?

How many successful authors today do you know who fit this description?

The answer, if you're unfamiliar with the business, is not many.

Or, uh, fewer than there used to be, anyway. Yes, there is still bad behavior in the publishing industry that goes unpunished or under-punished, but it will benefit your career to conduct yourself professionally.

Here are some tips.

IT PAYS TO HAVE SOCIAL SKILLS

Way back when, in simpler times, the book was what mattered. The author may have had to do some events and readings, but for the most part an author's engagement with the public was limited. Word of mouth, booksellers, and reviews drove sales. If a writer wrote a good book but was a pill to deal with, this was basically okay because they weren't really talking to many people.

Not so much anymore.

Now, with social media, TV, radio, and lots more travel, the author is face to face with their readership more than ever before. They're also being relied upon more and more to generate their own sales opportunities. All of this requires social skills. It helps when people want to work with an author because they're an awesome, friendly, professional, hardworking person.

Is a publisher going to decline to publish a fantastic book simply because the author is a jerk and a handful? Well, probably not, to be honest with you, and every year there's at least one headline-grabbing example of a bestselling writer behaving badly. But when difficult and nebulous decisions are being made in a publishing house, such as who gets which advertising budget, or if a publisher is unsure about whether to make a new offer, an author's attitude and behavior can be what tip the scales.

LET YOUR AGENT FIGHT YOUR BATTLES

Once your book sells to a publisher, you'll have a veritable new army of people to work with, from your editor to book designers to publicists.

Inevitably, something will happen on the way that will upset you or give you cause for concern. When this happens, **go straight to your agent.**

Don't try to deal with it yourself. This is why you're giving your agent 15% of your hard-earned cash. They're there to fight your battles and be the bad cop to your good cop. They're much better equipped to navigate thorny situations, to bring the hammer down if it needs swinging, and to talk you down if you're being the crazy one (ahem).

ERR ON THE SIDE OF TRANSPARENCY

Throughout your publishing journey, you'll be faced with numerous instances when you might not be sure how much to tell prospective agents, your actual agent, or your editor. You might have difficult or embarrassing situations in your personal life that arise, and you might be unsure whether, say, it would be professional to divulge this information to your agent or editor.

Err on the side of transparency, and again, go to your agent first. It's better to put the truth out there than to set up situations where the professionals you're working with are making decisions with incomplete information.

As an author, I was immensely relieved that I decided to tell my agent I was going through a divorce when I was completing the edits on one of my novels. She was extremely understanding and helped me push back a delivery date so that I could work at a slower pace during this time. Had I kept this private, I might have had a ton of extra stress to deal with.

It's better in the long run to be honest and transparent.

TRY TO ENJOY THE RIDE

Navigating the traditional publishing process can be really stressful and have lots of thorny decisions, painful rejections, bad reviews, events outside of your control, waiting, and unfortunate luck. Even when you find success, it's inevitably accompanied by some shiv in your side that makes the experience not quite as wonderful as you thought it was going to be. It can be surprisingly easy to forget that HOLY CRAP, YOU'RE PUBLISHING A FREAKING BOOK.

Try to keep your chin up, seek shelter with friends and family when you need it, remember the 10

Commandments of the Happy Writer in Rule #41, and trust that if things ever go south with one book, you'll be able to write another one that you love even more.

ALL ABOUT
SELF-PUBLISHING

Rule #26
REVIEW THE ECONOMICS OF SELF-PUBLISHING

So. You're ready to self-publish? First, let's do a quick check to make sure you can either afford it or have the time and inclination to do everything DIY.

Contrary to a still-prevalent myth, you don't need to pay to make a book available for sale, even for paperbacks! Amazon and others will happily make your book available for sale without asking you for an up-front investment.

Still, you probably need to plan to put down some cash if you're self-publishing. You probably will not want to handle every single task yourself and may want to farm out some of the tasks to freelancers.

We'll cover these steps in greater depth in subsequent rules, but here are the ballpark costs involved:

EDITING

- Developmental editing from a professional editor: $1,000-$5,000 or more depending on your book length
- Copyediting: $250–$1,000 depending on your book length

INTERIOR DESIGN

- $100–$500 depending on the complexity of your interior design (for instance, non-illustrated novels aren't very complicated, but the price will go up if you have graphs, charts, and/or illustrations)

COVER DESIGN:

- $100–$1,000

MARKETING

- $0–Infinity. This one really depends on your inclination and resources.

MISCELLANEOUS

- I'd plan to spend an additional $500 for smaller/unforeseen expenses, like ISBNs ($125 each), registering a copyright ($35), hiring other freelance help, like paying someone to write marketing materials or help with marketing ($50–$250), and/or fees if you choose to utilize Ingram Spark ($45).

Altogether, unless you're really pinching pennies and doing a lot of work yourself, I'd plan to spend a few thousand dollars.

HOW SELF-PUBLISHED AUTHORS MAKE MONEY

Now that we've gotten the expenses out of the way, here is the more pleasant part.

Here are the current splits from some of the major platforms when you publish through them directly. There are some additional wrinkles depending on the channels and where the books are sold, but here are the basic terms:

Amazon Kindle Direct Publishing:
- *Paperback*: 60% of the list price minus printing costs
- *Ebook*: 70% of the list price minus a "delivery cost" (an average of $0.06) if it's priced between $2.99 and $9.99; otherwise 35%

Barnes & Noble Press:
- *Paperback*: 55% list minus printing costs
- *Ebook*: 65% of the list price if it's priced above $2.99; otherwise 40%

Ingram Spark:
- *Paperback and ebook*: Varies. Check the comp calculator on their website

Kobo:
- *Ebook*: 70% of the list price if it's priced above $2.99

In addition to going direct to e-book retailers, there are also ebook distributors that will facilitate publication across many distributors. The two most prominent ones, as of this writing, are Smashwords and Draft2Digital. (These are also called "aggregators."). These distributors will make your ebook available in places that might be tricky to reach by yourself. (More on this in Rule #27.)

Here are the current splits.

Draft2Digital:
- *Ebook*: 10.5% of list price

Smashwords:
- *Ebook*: 10% of list price

DETERMINE YOUR BREAKEVEN POINT

Once you figure out the price for your print and e-book, you can determine the royalty you can expect per copy sold and then determine a rough estimate of how many copies you'd need to sell in order to cover your expenses.

It's very tricky, verging on impossible, to know how many copies you can expect to sell before you actually publish. You may not know going in whether it will be a money gainer or loser (and you may not particularly care much).

But before you start down the self-publishing path, take a hard look at the numbers, sleep on it, and make sure you feel comfortable moving forward.

Rule #27
CHOOSE YOUR FORMATS AND WHERE YOU WANT TO DISTRIBUTE

So! You want to pursue self-publishing. Here we go!

Now that you've made the decision, it's helpful to make two more as early as possible. First, you'll need to decide which formats you want to publish in. Print and e-books? Just e-books? If print, which kind of print: hardcover, paperback ... papyrus scrolls? Stone tablets?

Second, you'll need to figure out where to self-publish your book. Do you just want to go to Amazon for e-books? Do you want to have e-books available wherever e-books are sold? Who do you want to do the print edition?

"Wait a darn second here," you might be protesting. "Isn't the finished product the *last* step?"

It's important to decide where you're publishing as early as possible because the format(s) and distribution methods you choose influence several key steps in the self-publishing process:

- You'll need to design interiors (or have them designed) for the right print and e-book formats. Different e-book distributors have different file types.
- If you're publishing in print, you'll need to draft cover copy before you engage a designer so they'll know what to put on the back.
- The format will help decide the size of your eventual cover, which you'll also need to tell your cover designer.

Decide early and decide often!! Err ... scratch that. Decide early and TRY to decide only once. You can change your mind later, but you may have to repeat some steps.

So, let's walk through the options, shall we?

PRINT

If you decide to publish in print, you will have some decisions to make about which service(s) you go with. Some of the players include the following:

- **Kindle Direct Publishing** – This service, formerly known as CreateSpace, is owned by Amazon, and it's one of the easiest ways of getting your book in print. There aren't any up-front fees. However, as of this writing, they only offer paperback editions, and books with color cost more per copy. If you have a very design-heavy project, you may want to consider other options.
- **IngramSpark** – While IngramSpark costs a bit more up front (about $50 as of this writing), they offer a few more distribution and format options that may be of interest to people who are confident they'll be selling quite a few copies. Many libraries and booksellers are used to working with Ingram's wholesale service, so you may be more likely to achieve broader distribution through Ingram if your book begins to catch on.
- **Blurb** – Blurb's emphasis has historically been on design-oriented books, so if that's your jam, they may be a solid option for you.

Note that these choices aren't mutually exclusive. For instance, you can publish the paperback via **both** Kindle Direct Publishing and Ingram Spark in order to make it available on Amazon and also have it available via Ingram. (The quality of the print books will be virtually identical.)

The features offered by these services are constantly changing and there are tons of service providers in this space, so rather than try to give you a super-comprehensive rundown that might be out of date in two days, I'd just encourage you to shop around and check out the pros and cons for your particular project.

E-BOOKS VIA AMAZON

For e-books, Amazon's Kindle platform is by far the dominant format, to the point that in 2018 the online-sales database BookStat estimated Amazon represented more than 90% of e-book sales[1]. Just as with publishing in print, it doesn't cost anything up front to self-publish an e-book via Kindle Direct Publishing.

Amazon also offers authors some benefits for offering their book exclusively for sale on the Kindle platform, which is called Kindle Select. These include the following:

- Making your book available on Kindle Unlimited, Amazon's subscription reading service.
- A 70% royalty in some additional territories.
- Access to additional promotional tools, such as access to special discounting options.

---

1. https://www.idealog.com/blog/changing-book-business-seems-flowing-downhill-amazon/

Do you want to maximize your Amazon sales or do you want to make your book available more broadly? It's ultimately up to you and your goals for your book. It's tempting to make Kindle your one-stop shop, especially given how dominant it is, but you may want your book available in as many places as possible.

E-BOOKS BEYOND AMAZON

If you do decide you want to make your e-book available beyond Amazon, you have another decision to make. In order to make your book available on Apple Books, Nook, Kobo, Google Play, and other e-book platforms, you can go directly to the e-book retailers or go to an e-book distributor, like Smashwords, Draft2Digital, or Ingram Spark, that will make your book available in the other formats. Or you can combine the two and go directly to some retailers and otherwise distribute through Smashwords/Draft2Digital/Ingram Spark.

The advantage of going directly to the retailers is that you usually get a higher royalty. The disadvantage is that it takes a bit longer to get everything uploaded and you will have more places you need to monitor for sales and other updates.

For this guide, I published the print edition through both Kindle Direct Publishing and Ingram Spark, I published the e-books directly through Kindle, Nook, and Kobo, and I used Smashwords for Apple Books and other distributors, like Scribd.

I have largely been happy with my life choices.

Once you've made these key decisions, you're ready to move on to the next steps in your self-publishing journey. By having thought through these questions ahead of time, you'll be much more prepared for your voyage.

Rule #28
HAVE YOUR BOOK EDITED AT LEAST TWICE

As we discussed in Rule #3, there are two stages of editing a book, and you should treat them as separate and distinct: developmental editing and copyediting.

Developmental editing helps you improve the substance of your work, whether this is character development, plot arcs, and dialogue for fiction or structure and narrative voice for nonfiction. Copyediting refers to correcting all the typos and grammar errors and making sure that you're not going to embarrass yourself when your book is in the hands of readers.

Tackle developmental editing *before* you tackle copyediting. Why? It's pointless to pay someone to correct your typos when major sections are going to change in the course of the editing process. A copyeditor should be working with a manuscript that is substantively finished.

I'm not someone who believes that you necessarily *have* to pay someone for developmental editing. Good editors come in all shapes and sizes, and your edits can come from a paid editor, a critique partner, a friend, a spouse, a mortal enemy ... whoever they are, they should help you get your manuscript into better shape than you could achieve on your own. You should get help both from an overall structural perspective all the way down to line by line edits.

The advice should be positive, useful, strike you with the occasional "Why didn't I see that?!" moment, and, perhaps most importantly, should be consistent with your vision for the project. In other words, the person critiquing your work shouldn't simply be telling you how they would have written it.

Particularly with self-publishing, there can be some added benefit to working with a professional editor to be absolutely sure you're making the book as strong as possible before it goes on sale. (Feel free to reach out to me if you need help finding an editor: nathan@nathanbransford.com.)

Here are some pointers for working with a professional:

- **Don't spend money on a freelance book editor that you can't afford to lose.** If it feels like too much money, it is definitely too much money. Feedback is helpful, but not at the expense of funds that could be better used elsewhere. If you can spare it and it won't hurt a whit, go for it. Otherwise, there are plenty of free ways to get good feedback. A good freelance editor will cost from $1,000–$5,000 or more, depending on your book's length.

- **Check the editor's credentials.** Find out what their experience is, who they've worked with in the past, and whether the amount they are charging is commensurate with their experience. There are tons of great editors with extensive industry experience. Do your research, and only work with an editor with whom you are completely comfortable.

- **Know what you're paying for.** Make sure you have a very clear understanding of your goals, what you're paying for, and what you're getting.

- **Plan to be patient.** It usually takes a month or more to read and edit a whole manuscript. Work this into your publication timeline.

- **Be prepared to do the work.** The thing you *want* to hear ("This is the most amazing book ever written and you are a genius!! You don't need to change a word!") is the thing that is the least helpful to hear. Go into the process prepared to roll up your sleeves after you receive the feedback.

Unless you happen to have a friend who copyedits on a professional basis who owes you a favor, I would highly, highly recommend paying a copyeditor to work on your manuscript. You absolutely cannot have an end product that feels professional if it's riddled with typos and grammar errors. Copyediting will likely cost somewhere in the range of $250–$1,000, depending on your book length, and you can find copyeditors via online services, like New York Book Editors and Reedsy.

Even the best copyeditor will probably not spot every single typo or mistake, so even after they're finished, try to go through your manuscript several more times very slowly to try to catch everything. At the end of the day, you're the one who's responsible for the book you're releasing to the public.

Do not neglect developmental editing and copyediting! Once you've finished a book, it's so tempting to want to rush it out there to see what readers think and watch those sales come in. But, a well-edited book will reap massive dividends.

Resist the rush, put in the work when you receive feedback, and when you're all finished you'll be able to bask in the knowledge that you've done everything you can to make your book as strong as possible.

Rule #29
WRITE GOOD JACKET COPY

One of the most important tasks you'll tackle when you're self-publishing is coming up with a good description that will make someone want to buy your book. It's also helpful to do this before you start working with a cover designer so that you can provide them with the copy that will go on the jacket.

Writing good copy starts with preparation. It's important to know where your jacket and marketing copy will live and craft your pitch with that in mind. Since you're self-publishing, the copy on your physical book matters a lot less than how it's going to appear on Amazon and other marketplaces. Think less about your description as "jacket copy" and more as "marketing copy."

In order to write good marketing copy, you need to know why someone would want to read your book. For novels and narrative nonfiction, this means having a feel for what makes your plot compelling and unique in the market. For prescriptive nonfiction and how-tos, this means speaking to the key challenge your book is trying to solve as well as your authority to solve this particular problem.

Above all, it's crucial to know what makes your book stand out and hone in on this selling point. If your life depended on selling just one copy of your book, what would you say?

In online bookstores, you really don't have much room to grab someone. The "above the fold" jacket copy is vanishingly small—on Amazon it's about seven lines. You really need to make it count.

Luckily, if you followed Rule #5 on crafting a pitch, you should already have a good starting place for your jacket copy.

To review, for nonfiction, be crystal clear about what you're trying to solve and why you're the person to solve it. For fiction, lead with your one-sentence pitch:

When OPENING CONFLICT happens to CHARACTER(s), they have OVERCOME CONFLICT to COMPLETE QUEST.

Once you've nailed the opener, now it's time to provide more detail. For your physical book, talk to your cover designer about what length would mesh with the cover design and optimize with this in mind.

For your sales copy for the online marketplaces, you have much more space "below the fold" after those first seven lines. (But don't go on endlessly.)

If your book is nonfiction, you can either go into more detail about what you'll cover or use the space for blurbs that show your authority (which is what I opted to do for *How to Write a Novel*).

If you've written a novel, draw upon your two-paragraph pitch to flesh out more of the plot and world.

Also, jacket copy is a different beast than query letters! You can be a bit more of a hype machine (rather than just stick to the plot basics), it's fine to drift into themes a bit more, and avoid spoilers. You'll also need to mix in your credentials in a seamless way.

Even if this is your debut novel and you don't have a publishing credit to your name, give some thought to showing your authority. Solicit blurbs, try to get reviews from local media, show past reviews, or list other books you've written. Don't put credentials in just to put them in if they have nothing to do with your book, but the more you can do to show why you're the best person in the world to have written your book, the more copies you'll sell.

While it can be maddening to try to cram your selling points into a short seven-line summary, the good news is that when it comes to your sales copy, it's not set in stone. You have the opportunity to tweak it to see what works best. You can test different versions of your hook using Facebook ads and see which one has the best clickthrough or show a few different versions of your jacket copy to critique partners you trust.

You can always tweak the copy even after the book goes on sale, and you'll be able to see if a certain approach results in a sales bump. Try a few different approaches and see what works best.

Rule #30
DON'T NEGLECT YOUR INTERIOR DESIGN

When you think about self-publishing, you probably think about the writing, the cover, your marketing plan, and who's going to buy it. You might not be thinking about interior design. Yet, this is one of the most important steps in saving a book from looking amateurish.

If there's only one takeaway you get from this chapter, let it be this one: **don't neglect your interior design**.

Barring a serious money crunch or you're passionate about design and want to go DIY, I'd highly recommend hiring an interior designer to help you.

You can either reach out to me for help (nathan@ nathanbransford.com) or look for one in an online database like Reedsy.

It's helpful to undertake this step in tandem with your cover design (see the next Rule for more on cover design) because there is a bit of interplay between the two. Your cover designer will need to know the number of interior pages in order to design the print cover, and your interior designer may want to know what the cover looks like so that they can make the design of the interior cohesive with this look and feel. (This is why some designers offer one-stop-shop services.)

A good interior designer will save you from having to get deep into the formatting weeds. The interior design process always ends up being trickier and more time consuming than you want it to be. There are several different e-book and print formats for various distributors, and you'll need files for each of them.

Finding someone with an eye for interior design is key. You may well be able to figure out how to export your book into the right formats for self-publishing, but are you going to choose a good font? Are you going to manage some of the formatting quirks within your book so that everything looks polished?

I hired someone when self-publishing my guide to writing a novel and this very book you are reading right now, and it's one of the best decisions I've made.

The interior looks clean and polished in any format and looks unique rather than cookie-cutter.

Chef's kiss

Otherwise, there are more options for formatting your own interior design than ever before.

Word processing programs like Scrivener, Pages, and even good old-fashioned Microsoft Word will let you format and export your book into both e-book and print-friendly formats. Sites like Reedsy have exporting options, programs like Vellum let you customize your design, and Amazon has a formatting service for Kindle.

Rather than giving you a rundown of every single option out there, my recommendation is to start with the word processing program you're most comfortable with and then research how to make the leap from that format to the e-book and print formats you're planning to publish in.

Whatever you do: **double- and triple-check the formatting**

Once again for the rafters: your interior formatting will make a world of difference in the professionalism of your self-publishing effort.

The self-publishing platforms will all give you a preview of how your book will look when it's published. Scour these for errors, and if you don't trust your own eye for design, get a fancy friend to help you.

Don't skimp on this step.

Rule #31
GET YOURSELF A GOOD COVER

One of the very best parts of the self-publishing process is that you get to choose your own cover. Revolutionary, I know!

In the traditional publishing process, authors almost never have approval over their cover, and it's even somewhat rare to have meaningful consultation over what it looks like. For some authors, it can feel like "consultation" is limited to telling the editor how much you love your cover. I was fortunate enough to really love my covers for the *Jacob Wonderbar* series, but just about every other author I know has gone through cover hell with a publisher at one point or another.

Here's how I went about creating my cover for *How to Write a Novel*, which I used as a template for this guide as well.

FIND A DESIGNER

You may well have an eye for design, or maybe you have a talented designer friend who can help you with this. My design skills are terrible, so I needed help. Over drinks, my friend Mari Sheibley mentioned that she was working on a cover for a university press, and I asked her if she'd do the cover for my guide to writing a novel. She is a fabulously talented graphic designer, the brains behind early Foursquare badges and other influential internet design (she was even name-dropped on HBO's *Silicon Valley*).

She said yes, and a few weeks later I had concepts.

If you don't have a ready and willing friend, there are lots of designers out there on databases like Reedsy or Upwork who can help you out for a reasonable fee. As with any other freelancer, check their credentials thoroughly.

CONSIDER THE THUMBNAIL

You might be thinking about your cover in terms of great art or what would look fancy on a bookshelf. You might not be thinking about what it's going to look like as a small icon on someone's phone., but it pays to consider the modern shopping experience, especially when you're self-publishing.

When I was self-publishing my guides, I knew I wanted my title and my name to be readable even if the cover was just a thumbnail so that it would pop as people are browsing on Amazon and Barnes & Noble.

I also knew for branding purposes and for general favorite-color reasons that I wanted to debut with an orange color palette. Those were my only two requirements. I left the rest up to Mari.

ENVISION HOW IT WOULD LOOK IN AN E-BOOKSTORE

As you're deciding between cover concepts, it might be difficult to choose.

One really easy way to help you decide is to go on Amazon, search for books that are similar to yours, and take a screenshot.

Then copy your cover concept(s) in and see how it looks among your competitors. This is especially important if you're working in a specific genre. You want to know how your book is going to look among the crowd.

When I did this step, it was totally apparent which concept popped more. I went with the one that featured more orange. It was wonderfully clarifying.

It may be difficult to let go of some of the more artistic cover ideas you dreamed up while you were writing your book, but if sales are important to you, it's very important to consider how you'll stand out from the crowd online.

Rule #32
CONSIDER PUBLISHING AN AUDIOBOOK

Many people these days like to read their books with their ears, and you might be surprised just how easy it is to get an audiobook out there. It's totally possible to self-publish an audiobook and reach readers in this fast-growing format. I did just that with my guide to writing a novel, which you can find at your local online audiobook retailer.

There are two main questions that will help you determine the path to take when self-publishing an audiobook: Do you want to narrate yourself or do you want to hire a narrator?

And do you want to make your book available exclusively via the currently dominant player ACX (which distributes to Amazon/Apple/Audible) or do you want wider distribution via a company like Findaway (which makes your audiobook available to a burgeoning audiobookselling landscape that includes Google Play, Nook Audio, Overdrive, and others)?

The answers to these questions will help determine how you go about producing the files, where you will sell them, and the royalties you will receive.

It can be tricky to decide whether you want to read or not. Chances are you find the idea of someone else reading your book out loud a little strange, but consider this: it is very difficult, exhausting, and time consuming to read your own audiobook, and there are professionals out there who are wildly good at it.

A very, very rough rule of thumb is that every 10,000 words on the page results in one hour of finished audio. If you're an inexperienced audiobook reader, accounting for breaks and do-overs, you should plan to spend at least two-three hours reading for every finished hour of audio. So, if you have an 80,000 word novel, you should plan to spend about 24 hours recording. This really adds up!

To produce a good audiobook, you also need to produce it in a soundproof space that will result in a high-quality recording. Audiobook distributors check to see if your recordings meet their standards, so don't even waste your time recording in a loud space.

It's also helpful to have someone who knows what they're doing on hand to make you sound good and then stitch together the final product out of all of your stutters and do-overs. There are lots of local studios who offer this, so check your area for resources.

Unless you're an expert or are super into learning new skills, I'd highly recommend hiring a professional studio to produce your audio, which will likely run you from $250–$1,000 or more per finished hour, depending on how quickly you're able to get through the material with all the do-overs.

If, however, you want to find a voice that's as great as your book, both ACX and Findaway offer services to connect you with narrators who are integrated with their platforms. On ACX, you also have the opportunity to try to find a narrator who will work on a royalty split, which won't cost you anything up front. Outside of the distributors, there are many other places you can cast an audiobook narrator, including John Marshall Media, Voices, Upwork, or your favorite local freelance voice actor.

If you're paying a narrator up front, you should plan to spend $100–$400 per finished hour on a narrator. It's helpful to have a sense of the type of reader you want beforehand so that you can articulate this to the narrators who will produce a brief audition. Then, after you have some auditions, choose the one who you feel is best for your book and work out a deal.

When you're ready to start recording, you need to work on an audiobook script that adds any introductory material you want, swaps out all mentions of things like "reading more" for "listening more," and includes a wrap-up that includes, at minimum, "The End" so that the listener knows the audiobook is over (which is mandatory for the audiobook distributors).

Then, once everything is recorded and edited and you have the digital files, you're ready to get everything uploaded. As of this writing, it takes around three weeks from the time the files are uploaded for the audiobook to go on sale.

It's tricky to make the economics of self-publishing an audiobook work, so before you start down this path, get a sense of the costs and how many copies you'd need to sell to break even based on the path you choose, and do a gut check to make sure it makes sense for you.

Rule #33
DETERMINE YOUR PRICE POINT AND GET IT UPLOADED

The control and flexibility that self-publishing affords writers is a wonderful thing. Nowhere is this power more apparent than with setting your price point and making it available for sale.

Want to experiment with the price? Create a discount for a promotion? The self-publishing world offers a great deal of flexibility. The important thing to remember with your price point is that nothing is set in stone. You can shed your stress and start thinking strategically because you can change the price if you need to.

GET IN TOUCH WITH YOUR GOALS

Reflect a little bit on what you're hoping to achieve with your book.

Do you want to build up your name recognition and reach a wide audience? Might want to go for a lower price point because readers are more likely to take a chance on a new writer if it doesn't cost them too much.

Do you want to maximize your revenue? Might want to go a little higher.

Do you want to be a symbol of everything that's wrong with the world? Make one copy, charge a million dollars, and see which nefarious cartoon villain buys it!

Your book might even be incidental to your ultimate goals. You might be using it as a brand-builder for a speaking career or a separate commercial enterprise, which could mean a lower or higher price point depending on what you're going for.

You just have to decide on an initial pricing model that works for you, and you can always change things later if you want to experiment.

RESEARCH THE COMPETITION

This is a no-brainer. See what others are charging and know where you'll be positioned in the marketplace. You can either go with the flow, undercut, or aim a little higher, but this is crucial information for you to know where you stand.

It's also important to remember that the royalty rates vary based on your price point and to make sure you're hitting a sweet spot. For instance, as of this writing, Amazon offers 70% royalties for e-books that are priced between $2.99 and $9.99 but 35% royalties for e-books priced outside of this band.

GET SOME FEEDBACK

Bounce around your ideas, and if you have a community, try to talk to them, too. Get a sense of what "feels" right to people.

I took a poll when I was launching *How to Write a Novel*, and the community's vote of $4.99 matched my hunch, so I went with this.

TAKE AN EDUCATED GUESS WHEN YOU LAUNCH AND START EXPERIMENTING

Don't overthink it. You're not locked into a price, you can change as you go. So, you can start trying out different price points.

Gauge the impact of changes in price on your sales until you settle into a sweet spot. These can be as a temporary discount that you actively promote, or you can just quietly change the price and see if it impacts sales.

If you publish via Kindle Direct Publishing, Amazon also has a tool that will gauge your optimal price point relative to your subject matter and sales over time. You can use that for further inspiration for experiments.

Then, keep checking your numbers. See how things are going relative to your goals. If you just want your book out there, your KPI (key performance indicator) is your sales. If you are maximizing for money, your KPI is your revenue. If you are maximizing for reputation, your KPI may be your reviews.

As you can probably tell, this isn't rocket science. Don't agonize. Just know what you want, know what you're measuring, and experiment until you're in the sweet spot.

Rule #34
UPLOAD YOUR FILES

You're almost there!

At this point, you should have your interior files, your cover images, your marketing copy, and your initial prices. Now there are just a few final steps to make your books available for sale.

CONSIDER GETTING AN ISBN

An ISBN is a 13-digit code that's used by book-stores, libraries, and distributors to identify a book. ISBNs cost around $125 per book format in the United States (meaning: print and audio editions of the same book need separate ISBNs). You can purchase these through Bowker either individually or in a bulk batch at a discount.

If you're self-publishing, getting an ISBN is actually an optional activity because many platforms like Amazon don't require one, and other distributors will give you either an ISBN or a separate identification number for free or at a discount. However, there are some advantages to purchasing your own ISBN. Retailers won't sell books without an ISBN, and if you ever want to change distributors or if you have broader ambitions as a publisher, an ISBN can help keep your books unified under the same identification number and ensure that you are always listed as the publisher. (Note: if you get a free identification from a distributor like IngramSpark, they will probably be listed as the publisher, not you.)

I ultimately decided to purchase ISBNs for my self-published books, but if your ambitions are limited or you're sticking to e-books, you may ultimately decide against it to save some cash.

CHOOSE YOUR CATEGORIES AND KEYWORDS

When you upload, you'll likely need to choose some categories and keywords in order to help the bookseller know where to list your book.

For fiction, it's usually pretty straightforward to hone in on your category or genre, but there are lots of different permutations for nonfiction, so you may want to spend some time researching books that are similar to yours on Amazon and Barnes & Noble to see how they are categorized.

For the keywords, put yourself in the shoes of someone who is searching for a book like yours. If you wrote a fantasy novel, you might choose "Dragons," "Knights," "Magic," etc., while if you wrote a diet book, you might choose keywords like "Diet," "Fitness," "Health," etc.

UPLOAD!

This may just be the easiest step out of this whole process.

You'll need to upload your files and enter the marketing copy in all the different places that you're planning to distribute. Be very careful to make sure you're choosing the right options (be especially careful to choose the right option for Amazon exclusivity or nonexclusivity), but overall the sites are pretty self-explanatory and straightforward.

You can either set the publication date in the future or publish immediately. Your book will be under review for 24–72 hours, and then you'll have a book that's available for sale.

WHOA! YOUR BOOK IS PUBLISHED!

If you notice a typo in your book or want to make a change after it's published, don't sweat it, you can correct the error and upload new files. Down the line, if you ever decide you want to unpublish your book or create a new edition, you can remove your books for sale at any time.

NOW GET YOUR COPYRIGHT REGISTERED

There are lots of misconceptions around copyright and what it means. One important thing to understand: your work is copyrighted the minute you create it. You don't need to put a copyright symbol on every page or do anything special.

However, there are additional legal advantages conferred by *registering* your copyright with the Library of Congress within three months of publication. It makes it easier to sue for damages if someone ends up infringing on your work.

To register, go to copyright.gov and follow the instructions.

As I believe I have mentioned before, I am not an attorney, so please consult with one if you are unsure.

Rule #35
MAKE THE LEAP FROM SELF-PUBLISHING TO TRADITIONAL (IF YOU WANT TO)

Once you've self-published, you may entertain some ideas about potentially making the leap to traditional publishing. So, let's get this out of the way: Does self-publishing kill your chances of finding a traditional publisher someday?

No. Not by a long shot.

The days of literary agents and publishers sneering at self-published authors is long, long gone. There are extremely successful authors who started via self-publishing, extremely successful authors who started with a traditional publisher and now self-publish, and extremely successful authors who do a mix of both.

There is not a self-publishing stigma. If you want to try to make the leap from self-publishing to traditional publishing, the fact that you self-published isn't necessarily going to hold you back.

HOWEVER. There is still a self-publishing *skepticism*.

As in, literary agents and publishers know that many books that are self-published landed there because they did not meet the threshold of quality and craft that lends itself to traditional publication. They will definitely consider self-published authors, but you may have some convincing to do that your books are diamonds in the rough instead of, well, just rough.

So, what do literary agents look for in an author who previously self-published?

It's tough to generalize across all agents and book projects because situations differ so much, but on the whole, agents don't just want to see that you self-published a book and maybe sold some copies. They want to see if you self-published *well*.

Did you write a really good book? Were you a great "Book CEO" and assembled a solid cover, interior design, and marketing plan? Did your book attract genuinely good reviews? Were you able to gain some local media attention, and/or have you parlayed it into a strong social media presence?

An author who has demonstrated great taste, determination, and grit is the type of author a literary agent wants to work with.

Most importantly of all: Are you a darn good writer? Agents are looking for someone they can build up over the long haul. They want to know that you're hungry and talented.

There are two scenarios in which you might consider approaching agents: when you have a self-published book that is beginning to take off (meaning: sales that are at least in the thousands) or you've written an entirely new book.

APPROACHING AGENTS WITH A SELF-PUBLISHED BOOK

When agents and publishers are considering taking on a book that was initially self-published, they want to know that the book has untapped potential. Did your book sell very well relative to you being an unknown, but the book's potential hasn't yet been tapped out?

If you can imagine a curly line on a graph, your chances increase the more you sell, but then there's a bit of a tapped-out valley until you've sold so much that you've reached phenomenon level and your chances go up again.

Publishers will only want to take on a previously self-published book if they believe they can do something to increase the sales. If a publisher feels you have already maximized your natural reach within your genre, they might conclude there's not much more they can do for you. That is, until your book begins to catch fire outside the hardcore readers of your genre and your book seems like it has limitless potential.

How do you know you've reached phenomenon status? Well, by this point publishing people will probably be approaching you rather than the other way around.

(Also, by this point you may well wonder why you need a traditional publisher entirely.)

But, even if you have an existing project with potential, it still helps to have a new book.

APPROACHING AGENTS WITH A NEW BOOK

As literary agent Sarah LaPolla told me:

"If you already self-pubbed 100 books and you're approaching an agent, be prepared to send them a project that's all-new, never-been-published, that they will be able to send to traditional publishers while helping you manage your previously self-published backlist."

Starting fresh with a new project can be a helpful way of breaking out from self-publishing to traditional publishing.

And yes, this often doesn't just mean a new project, it also means steering away from a self-published series. This is because it's ridiculously difficult to convince a publisher to take on a sequel to a self-published book.

There are lots of reasons for this, everything from publishers wanting to make as much of a splash launching a book as possible to the inevitable series sales drop-off effect: every installment of a series tends to sell incrementally less than the first book.

There are exceptions to this, but in general, if you really want to make the leap to a traditional publisher, it helps to be starting fresh with a new world.

Don't get so caught up in one series that you stop believing you can create another.

HOW TO MAXIMIZE YOUR CHANCES OF FINDING AN AGENT

So ... ready to start querying literary agents as a self-published author? Here's how to maximize your chance of success:

- **Be clear in your query that you previously self-published**. If you are querying for a previously self-published book and not a new project, be sure to list the sales (again, they should at least be in the thousands). Sales aren't quite as important if you are querying for a new project, but you should still list your previously self-published books.

- **Mention any media coverage you received.** This includes interviews, real reviews (i.e., don't include any reviews that you paid for), or any notable attention you were able to drum up.
- **You don't need to be overly detailed as you describe your previous books**. This is because you want to …
- **Keep the query focused on your new project**. You want to get an agent genuinely excited about your next book. Even if you've done very well self-publishing, you still have to make the project you're querying about sound as awesome as possible. Keep the focus there.
- **Write a really good query letter.** Review the tips in Rules #12–15 and really nail this letter. Don't assume your past projects are going to carry the day.

There are so many different paths that authors can take these days, and it can be difficult to decide whether to go traditional or to self-publish. At the end of the day, if you self-publish first and still want to be traditionally published, your best strategy is to self-publish well and write another good book.

PROMOTING YOUR BOOK AND STAYING SANE ON YOUR PUBLISHING JOURNEY

Rule #36
THE KEY TO MARKETING: DO WHAT YOU'RE BEST AT

There are two powerful and enduring myths out there about book marketing that—spoiler alert—are both wrong.

First, there was once a mystical era of book publishing where writers just wrote and magical book marketing elves took care of the rest. NOPE. The second is that writers need to do every single thing under the sun and make book marketing a second full-time job. ALSO NOPE.

Writers have always needed to find ways to market themselves and their writing, and this was as true for Lord Byron as it is for you, the modern author. Writers like Lord Byron, Oscar Wilde, Mark Twain, Ernest Hemingway, and Ayn Rand were among the best networkers and self-promoters of their day.

This holds whether you are going down the traditional publishing path or you're self-publishing. It pays to be a good marketer.

But, you don't have to do it all. In fact, what if I told you there are only two things you really need to do?

Every author, published or unpublished, should have some sort of Google-able web presence so that when someone sees your work or hears about you, they have a way to contact you. (More on this in Rule #37.) And these days, every author should have some sort of social media presence. (More on this in Rule #38.)

Beyond these basic requirements, there's a false conventional wisdom out there that the key to being a Good Hardworking Promoting Author is to blow out your blog, your Facebook page, your website, your Twitter feed, your Instagram, your Goodreads network, and better yet all the above, and by the way you also need to set up your own author tour and try to get some media appearances going and place some articles and stories while you're at it and where's your book trailer oh also don't quit your day job and don't forget about your manuscript deadline and make sure the next book is incredible and amazing and could you spend some time with your family please?

Needless to say, unless you were born with more hours in the day than the rest of us, doing everything is impossible.

Nor is doing everything productive! If you don't have a passion for blogging, it's going to show. Readers will notice, and your blog will remain obscure. Not a newsflash: obscure blogs don't sell books.

No one should be blogging (or Tweeting or Facebooking or etc.) for the sake of blogging (or Tweeting or Facebooking or etc.).

It takes time to create a good blog, a good Twitter feed, an artful Instgram account, a good Facebook page, a good book trailer, etc., and if you dilute your time and try to do *everything*, you might end up without a good *anything*.

Instead: **do what you're best at.** Don't make yourself miserable doing what you think you *should* be doing, do what you *enjoy* doing. Do what you're skilled at doing.

Utilize your time where it's best spent. If you have a talent and passion for blogging, do this. If you enjoy Twitter and know the ins and outs, do this. If you like getting into the weeds of Facebook or Google or Amazon ads and A/B testing the best messaging, do this.

There's no one way to promote a book, and if there were a surefire way to get a book to take off and become a massive bestseller, I would patent it and sell it to you for seven trillion dollars. Know your strengths, utilize your time well, and remember that at the end of the day the whims of fate and word of mouth are more powerful than any marketer.

Need some ideas? Here's a list of marketing tactics. Don't try to do everything on this list, just hone in on two or three or however many you can manage *well*.

ONLINE BOOK MARKETING IDEAS

- **Paid advertising** – Many self-published authors have had success with ads on Amazon, Facebook, Google, BookBub, and others. There's a learning curve, and it's easy to lose money if you're not smart about it, but it can also be very effective. (David Gaughran has great resources on his website if this is a direction you're curious about.)

- **Blogging** – Yes, people still read blogs. It's a bit harder to build an audience than it used to be, but if you provide value and stick with it, you can still reach people.

- **Content marketing** – Pitch articles to national publications and popular blogs. Make sure what you're pitching is aligned with a topic that makes sense for the publication, and don't just do something boilerplate.

- **Podcasting** – Sure, it seems like everyone under the sun has a podcast these days, but it's still a growing market. If you have a good one, people will find you.

- **YouTube** – YouTube is famously the world's second biggest search engine after Google. Especially if you are working in a visual arena or you have a killer idea for a book trailer, YouTube can be a strong platform.

- **Newsletter** – Good old-fashioned email is still a tried and true way of reaching an audience. Think creatively about how you'll make your newsletter stand apart and how you'll capture subscribers.

- **Engage with message boards and online groups** – This doesn't work if you're going to just spam a board, but if you organically belong to some online communities, think about how you can engage with them to promote your book.

- **Solicit review**s – DO NOT pay for fake reviews, but do make sure to remind people how much reviews matter.

- **Giveaways** – Host a giveaway on your blog or social media profiles to draw attention to your book release.

- **Blog tours** – Reach out to top bloggers to arrange a series of posts around publication time.

- **Author marketing collectives** – Join forces with other authors who are releasing their books around the same time to multiply your reach.
- **Price promotions** – Drop your price for a limited time to create a sales boost.
- **Engage with influencers** – Reach out to top book reviewers and influencers to try to solicit posts and reviews.
- **Host a webinar** – Have something that you can teach the world or better yet that ties in with your book? Teach a class or host a free webinar.
- **Alumni network** – Your university or high school may be excited about what you're up to.
- **Add a link in your email signature** – Think about how many emails you send. Now think of how many more people could be aware of your book.
- **Crowdfund** – Some successful books get their start on Kickstarter and other crowdfunding platforms, which gets people invested in a book before its release.
- **Email your friends** – Don't forget to tap into your personal network. Your friends and acquaintances may be able to give your book a boost.

OFFLINE BOOK MARKETING IDEAS

- **School visits** – Talking to a bunch of kids can be wildly terrifying, but some children's book authors are fantastic at translating their books to successful school visits.

- **Local and national media** – If you're really well-networked you can perhaps parlay these connections into appearances on local or national media. People still watch TV, read the newspaper, and listen to the radio, you know.

- **Bookstore appearances and signings** – It can be a bit tricky to convince bookstores to stock and feature you, especially if you're a self-published author, but with some gumption you can successfully pound the pavement.

- **Local stores and coffee shops** – Bookstores aren't the only places people buy books! Other stores in your community may be willing to sell your book.

- **Conferences and festivals** – Pitch workshops or speaking topics to writers conferences or trade events.

- **Solicit and deploy blurbs from successful authors** – These tend to evolve organically, and I don't recommend spamming every author under the sun, but do at least try with the ones you know.

- **Tie-ins** – Can you associate your book with other products or newsworthy events? Would museums or galleries be interested in your book?
- **Partnerships** – Are there companies who you might be able to partner with to give you a boost?
- **Wacky events** – Po Bronson once staged a mock IPO for his novel Bombardiers and paid out shares of the hardcover sales. If you're a great party planner, do something that ties in!
- **Print and physical media advertising** – Yes, this is still a thing.
- **Donations** – Give your book away to people who need it. Not only will you be doing good, you might build lasting connections.
- **Swag** – Create some branded doo dads to give away to people. Bookmarks, book plates, t-shirts, keychains, you name it.

At the end of the day, you have to do what you can in the time you have. Just be smart about it.

Rule #37
BUILD A GOOD WEBSITE

Building a website may not exactly feel like it's something that belongs in the ole writer-skills toolkit, but I'm of the belief that it's extremely important.

Your website doesn't have to be elaborate, it doesn't have to be wildly inventive, and if you have a unique name, you might be able to get away with just having a Twitter account or some other means of being identifiable on the Internet.

And yes, this post goes for both the traditionally published and self-published. Everyone seeking publication or planning to self-publish would benefit from having one.

First, let me be clear: you don't *have* to have a website. Website-less authors are not summarily rounded up and disqualified from seeking publication. I'm sure you can name a bestselling author who is happily website-less.

But, it helps.

On the broader point of "Why can't authors just write," as I mentioned in the previous chapter, people often harken back to apocryphal golden eras of yore where authors could just be authors, often pointing to authors like Hemingway … who were actually wildly good self-promoters for their time.

You're a writer. You want people to read your book. Why would you cede the responsibility to market it to someone else?

You don't have to do everything yourself (including, ahem, building your website), and writing a great book is still the most important factor in your eventual success. But, you do need to take responsibility for marketing.

A website is a bare-minimum way of putting yourself out there.

Are you ready for the list of author website absolute must-haves?

- Your name
- A biography (doesn't have to be elaborate)
- A way to contact you

THAT'S IT.

It can literally just be one static page on the Internet. All you're really doing is giving people a means of learning more about you and getting in touch with you if, say, someone comes across something you've written or just wants more background and they Google your name.

That being said, while this is the minimum, it's better to try to include just a bit more in order to convey a sense of professionalism.

A good website can do more than just exist on the Internet. It's really an opportunity to connect with people that you may want to work with or people who may want to read your books.

There are two main elements of a good website:

- **Style** – Take some time to consider the design of your site. Style provides an important first impression. Good design inspires a sense of professionalism and prompts curiosity. If this isn't your strong suit, find someone to help you. Even if you can't afford a designer, think of who you might be able to barter with or how you can get creative about asking for help.

- **A reason to visit** – If you want people to return to your site and build a relationship with you, think about why someone might visit and what you want them to do when they arrive. Are you giving great information via a blog or resources? Is it a fun experience? Does someone who visits your site know what to do and where to find things?

Here's a checklist of things to include in a well-developed site:

- Your bio
- Your books, if you've published (I recommend that you keep things vague if you're unpublished and trying to find a literary agent)
- How and where to connect with you on social media
- Your blog, if you have one
- Your newsletter, if you have one
- Events and news, if you have events and are newsworthy
- How to contact you

It's so important to give people a way to find and connect with you. When I was a literary agent, there were so many times I read something I liked and then struggled to track down the author so that I could ask them what they were working on or pitch a book idea to them.

Don't miss an opportunity to be discovered! Build a good website.

Rule #38
UTILIZE SOCIAL MEDIA

Let me tell you a story about how I joined Twitter.

I didn't join it at all.

In 2008, someone created a fake profile for me, photo and all, and started tweeting out my blog posts! People were replying to me and everything. Once I got wind of what was happening, I wrested control of the account and grumpily determined it was time to succumb to this whole social media thing.

So, yes. I now have ~90,000 Twitter followers and social media eventually became the foundation of my professional career, but I can also relate to the deep reluctance some authors have to engage with social media.

But, take it from me: it pays to be active on social media. Even if you don't want to.

It doesn't have to be your life, it doesn't have to be an endless time waster, and you can be active on your own terms, but you should have a good, solid social media presence if you want to raise your platform as an author.

Here's a guide for social media for authors. Rather than focusing on specific platforms, which change and evolve quickly, here are some overall principles that I trust will remain timeless.

"Sure," you might say, "someone who had social media foisted upon them involuntarily in 2008 might have benefitted from it, but people like you had a 10-year head start! How could I possibly catch up?"

It's never too late.

In many ways, social media is still in its infancy, and there are always new accounts catching fire and plenty more people who don't have wildly successful accounts but who benefit from simply being active.

"But wait!!" you might be protesting (I treasure our imaginary conversations), "I'm not a published author. I have nothing of value to tweet about."

Not true. There are many unpublished authors who gained traction on social media by being super smart and engaging.

Camryn Garrett is Exhibit A. Over the last few years, she posted such smart things and engaged with authors in such a genuine way that she was soon on nearly everyone's radar in the publishing industry.

She got a hot book deal while she was still a teenager!

There's no time like the present. Get going.

One of the most under-appreciated elements of being active on social media is that it's a terrific tool for learning more about the publishing industry. Follow the agents who represent your favorite books. Follow your favorite authors. Follow publishing experts. Participate in discussions. You'll be surprised how quickly you'll come across interesting articles about the business and how much you'll learn through osmosis.

Also, pay attention to what works on social media. Don't necessarily imitate, as it pays to be yourself, but think about what it is about popular accounts that contributes to their success.

You don't have to join and be active on every social media platform. You'll likely go crazy if you try to do that, or you might suddenly wake up and find you've morphed into a Kardashian.

Instead, focus on the social media platforms you actually enjoy.

Better yet, if it's important to you to build a following, think about the reason someone should follow you. How are you providing value?

For instance, my following on Twitter has never really been about how witty or clever I am on Twitter. Instead, I'd wager most people follow me as a way of keeping up with my blog, which is my true social media "base." That's the real value I provide people.

Other people on social media are hilarious, while some are master curators and share all the best articles, some are very engaging and spark interesting conversations, some are wildly stylish, and some have the best takes on popular reality shows.

Find your niche and stick with it consistently for a while, converse with other people in your area, and you'll soon find your audience.

If there's anything I can leave you with, it's this: social media is social.

Seems simple, and ... it really is. Social media is all about what you make of it. If you're having fun, chances are your followers will have fun. If you're not having fun, take a break!

I've met some of my best IRL friends through social media, it's become a guiding light in my career, and I've enjoyed most of the time I spent on it.

So ... THANK YOU to the person who started my fake Twitter profile and forced me to join. I had no idea what a wonderful ride it would be.

Rule #39
PONDER THE RANDOMNESS OF BESTSELLERS

In the ocean there's a real phenomenon called rogue waves. They typically occur far out at sea, and they are almost entirely random occurrences. Suddenly a wave can appear out of nowhere and grow to a spectacular height. They're impossible to predict and extremely powerful.

This is about as good of a metaphor for bestsellers as I can think of.

It's very, very tempting to look back on bestsellers as preordained phenomena, but I really don't believe that's the case. There are some books, like *Harry Potter*, that pull off the Beatles feat of being both extremely good and extremely popular. There are others that just seem to capture the zeitgeist. But, for the most part, when we point to whatever it is that made something more popular than all the rest, we're benefitting from the magic of hindsight.

When you look at many mega bestsellers ... let's face it, a lot of them are head-scratchers. There are books that undeniably tap into something compelling, but the more books you read, both bestsellers and undiscovered gems, the more difficult it is to pinpoint *why* the big ones become big and some small ones stay small.

There are more sophisticated and edgier books than *Girl with the Dragon Tattoo,* for example. Why was *this* the one to take off?

There were a whole lot of dog memoirs before *Marley and Me.* Why this one?

Even the paths to publication don't have a huge amount in common. There's a spectrum, from "A lot of people saw it coming and the publisher paid accordingly" books like *Twilight* to "Where did that come from?" books like *Fifty Shades of Grey* that seemed to come out of nowhere.

Why do some books seem to ride a golden path and some clobber their way to the top? How do some books achieve a surge of momentum all the way through to *megabestsellerdom*?

Ask the waves.

There are only a few things you can do in the face of this randomness: write the best book you can, query widely if you're pursuing traditional publishing, and publish as best you can if you're self-publishing. Then, do everything in your power to market your book.

And don't let the randomness of massive success discourage you.

Rule #40
KNOW YOUR PUBLISHING TERMINOLOGY

There are a ton of terms that are unique to the publishing industry, and knowing the lingo is important! You need to understand what you're signing, what your agent is telling you, and what to expect.

Don't be afraid to ask your agent or another publishing professional to clarify an unfamiliar term or concept because even publishing veterans trip up on some of these.

Here's a glossary that might help:

Advance - The money a publisher pays an author to publish their book. This money is an advance against royalties. This means that the author does not receive additional money from the publisher until the book earns an amount of money equal to the advance (see "earn out"). As long as the book is published, the author does not have to pay the advance back, even if the book does not earn out. Large advances are typically paid in installments, such as a portion on signing, a portion on delivery and acceptance, and a portion on publication. Advances range from $1–$1,000,000 or more.

Agent - A publishing professional who shepherds books and authors through the publication process. An agent will submit a book project to editors, negotiate advances and contracts, follow-up on payments, and more generally serve as a creative and business adviser to an author (and much much more). An agent is the author's advocate.

ARCs – This stands for Advance Reading Copy. These are early editions of the book that are produced about six months in advance and are sent to buyers, reviewers, and influencers to drum up enthusiasm for a book. While terminology varies by publisher, ARCs are typically distinguished from bound galleys because they feature the actual cover of the book.

Association of Author's Representatives (AAR) – An organization of agencies who abide by a canon of ethics and host meetings and panel discussions to keep agents informed about trends and issues facing the industry.

Auction – When multiple publishing houses are interested in acquiring a project, they will sometimes bid against each other in an auction. While auction formats vary, typically the bids will proceed from lowest to highest and will last until one publisher has the highest bid and the others have dropped out. Auctions are a good thing for authors and agents.

Backlist – These are books that have been out for a while but whose rights publishers still possess.

Big Five – The five largest publishers: Penguin Random House, Simon & Schuster, HarperCollins, Hachette, and Macmillan.

Blurb - – A quote from an author or reviewer in praise of a book. Blurbs may or may not be on the cover of a book. Blurb is also the name of a prominent self-publishing company.

Book Expo – Still commonly known as "BEA" because it used to be called Book Expo of America. An annual, massive book convention in the US attended by publishers, agents, authors, librarians, bookstore reps, and anyone else with a connection to the book business.

Book plates – Stickers that go in the front of a book and often allow the owner of the book to sign their name. Book plates are a popular way for children's book authors to sign books (since book plates are very portable).

Bound Galleys – (see "Galleys")

British Commonwealth – A huge list of countries, territories, and exceedingly random islands, many of which you may not have known existed, which were often but not always colonized by Mother Britain. The British Commonwealth is important in publishing because it is often the countries and territories where British publishers will have exclusivity (see "Exclusivity"). To make it still more confusing, the list of British Commonwealth territories varies from publisher to publisher.

Buyer – The person at a bookstore or library who is responsible for ordering books that the store or library will carry on shelves.

Category – A broad grouping of books, roughly akin to the different sections of a bookstore. Not to be confused with genres, which are narrower and more specific.

Commission – The amount an agent receives for their services. Agents typically receive a commission of 15% for all domestic sales and 20% for foreign sales, which is split between the primary agent and a subagent (see "Subagent"). Agents only receive commission on works they sell, and thus they aren't paid unless the author is paid.

Co-op – You know those books at the front of Barnes & Noble? Those books didn't hitchhike there themselves: this placement is typically paid for by the publisher. Publishers make certain titles "available for co-op" and work out payment arrangements and special promotions, and it is then up to the bookstore to decide which titles get to go up front.

Copyeditor – A grammar and spelling ninja who is responsible for making sure books do not have typos, geographical errors, or dangling modifiers. Not to be confused with Editors.

Copyright – The legal right of ownership of a written work. Copyright in the US lasts for the author's life plus 70 years. Your work is technically copyrighted when you write it, although you want to make sure your publisher registers copyright of your work in your name with the Library of Congress within three months of its publication for additional legal protection.

Debut novel – An author's first published novel, not necessarily the first book they've written.

Deep discounts – When a publisher discounts steeply in order to move some books, they are often allowed to pay the author much, much less in royalties. Often a source of confusion and angst when royalty statements arrive.

Delivery and Acceptance (D&A) – The happy time when a publisher officially accepts a book for publication. This may trigger a D&A payment (see "Advance").

Delivery date – When your manuscript is due. Write it in the calendar in blood (but tell your agent if you think you're going to miss it).

Digital List Price (DLP) – In digital audio and e-book land, this is the price the publisher or rights holder places on a copy of their digital content. This may or may not have any bearing whatsoever on the price the e-publisher actually charges.

Distributor – The company that gets books from a publisher to bookstores, libraries, etc. Most major and some mid-major publishers function as their own distributors, while others use third parties (see "Wholesaler" for differentiation).

DRM – Digital Rights Management. This is software encryption that (theoretically) discourages piracy and which allows publisher to do fancy things like sync your e-book between your Kindle and your iPhone.

Earn out – When your book has earned more revenue than you were paid as an advance, it is said to have earned out. From here on out you get royalties on all net sales and all subrights income. Congratulations!

Editor – A publishing professional who works at a publishing house. An editor receives submissions (usually from agents), acquires projects, negotiates advances, and then coordinates with the different teams at a publisher throughout the publication process, such as production, sales, and marketing, basically making a book happen. An editor will typically be a savvy networker, have impeccable taste, and live in Brooklyn.

Editorial letter – The list of suggested changes an editor will ask an author to make prior to publication.

Not every single tiny suggestion must be taken, but an author would do well to please their editor.

Exclusivity – a) When an unpublished author gives an agent an "exclusive" look at their manuscript, usually for a period of time. This means the author cannot then send their manuscript to another agent during this time period. b) Exclusivity can also refer to the exclusive rights and territory that are granted to a publisher in a publishing contract (see also "Territory").

First pass pages – Once the manuscript is copy-edited, the pages are then type-set and designed to look how they'll look when the book is bound. A copy of these pages is then sent back to the editor and author, who check for any last errors that might have been missed or possibly introduced during the type-setting.

First proceeds – When a book is rejected for publication due to it being editorially unacceptable, some publishing contracts will allow the author to retain the advance and only repay the publisher out of the "first proceeds" from the sale to another publisher. Basically the author uses Publisher #2 to pay back Publisher #1.

First serial – Publication of an excerpt in a magazine or journal prior to book publication (see also "Second serial").

Flow through – In some contracts, when there is subrights income (see "Subrights"), the author's share of the revenue is allowed to "flow through" directly to the author without being held by the publisher until the end of a royalty period.

Front list – A publisher's books that have come out recently.

Galleys – These are early editions of the book that are produced about six months in advance and are sent to buyers, reviewers, and influencers to drum up enthusiasm for a book. While terminology varies by publisher, galleys are typically distinguished from ARCs by featuring a generic cover.

Genre fiction – A blanket term that refers to books with certain familiar settings and plot conventions. Genres include romance, science fiction, mystery and suspense, westerns, etc.

Hardcover – Books that are bound in cardboard or some other sturdy fashion, possibly featuring a dust jacket, and usually retailing at a higher price than paperbacks.

Imprint – The entity within a publisher whose name is printed on the spine of a book and which theoretically has a certain publishing "flavor." An imprint may be a division within a publishing house (Knopf, HarperCollins, etc.), it may be based around a certain genre (Harlequin Silhouette, Harlequin Blaze, etc.), or it may be a "boutique" imprint named after an editor(s) (Nan A. Talese, Balzer + Bray, etc.). Keeping imprints straight and remembering who reports to whom takes years of familiarity with the publishing industry and gigantic spreadsheets.

Indemnity – In a publishing contract, a publisher will typically require the author to indemnify the publisher against losses sustained due to a breach in the author's warranty (see also "Warranty"). In English: if the author screws up and plagiarizes someone or doesn't clear their permissions properly, the author is the one on the hook.

Indie or Independent publishing – There is a bit of a tussle within the business over what these words mean. Traditionally, indie publishing meant independent presses, the small publishers outside of the Big 5. But in the past 10 years, self-published authors have rather successfully appropriated the term "indie" to refer to self-publishing. So these days, the use of "indie" is pretty contextual. If it's someone who works in traditional publishing (or used to, like me), they're probably referring to small presses. If it's someone who self-published, they're probably referring to self-publishing.

ISBN – This stands for International Standard Book Number. It's a 13-digit code that serves as a unique identifier for a book, which is used by bookstores and libraries.

Joint accounting – In a multi-book publishing deal, joint accounting means the books need to earn out the entire advance with cumulative book sales in order for the author to earn out. This is distinct from separate accounting, where the books are accounted individually (see also "Earn out" and "Separate accounting").

Literary scout – A scout is someone who keeps tabs on all the hot books out there, usually on behalf of either film studios/producers or foreign publishers.

Mass market paperback – Rack-sized paperback. Basically the size you usually see at the grocery store.

Midlist – Midlist titles are those that are literally in the middle of the range of advances and sales on a publisher's list. Typically, midlist authors have a solid fan base but are not bestsellers. Some say the midlist is disappearing as publishers increasingly focus on their bestselling authors.

Narrative nonfiction – Nonfiction that illuminates through story, often centering around a central character or set of characters. Examples of narrative nonfiction include narrative history (*The Professor and the Madman* or *Devil in the White City*), true crime (*In Cold Blood* or *Helter* Skelter), memoir (*My Memoirs* by Insert Author), etc.

Net amount received – Usually the amount actually received by the publisher from sales of a work, sometimes also after taking out taxes and/or certain expenses (watch those contract definitions!).

Net sales – The number of actual sales after deducting returns. Also known as "sell through."

Nonexclusivity – When a publisher only has nonexclusive rights in a certain territory, the author may then grant these rights to another publisher.

North America – For the purposes of publishing terminology, usually refers to English speaking North America, i.e., the United States and Canada. Sorry, Mexico and Central America! Nothing personal.

Omnibus – When multiple books are collected into one volume, it's called an omnibus.

Open market – When rights have been granted exclusively in North America and the British Commonwealth, the rest of the world is typically considered an open market. This means that both the US and the British publisher may sell there.

Option – A provision in a contract that typically gives the publisher an exclusive period of time to consider and offer on the author's next work. The option may be limited or allow the publisher certain financial matching rights, so keep a close eye on this.

Out of print – When a book is no longer being actively sold by a publisher, it is said to be out of print, and often an author will be able to "revert" the rights. This term has gotten a little nebulous in the era of e-books and print on demand, so make sure your contract has a solid definition.

Partial – A partial manuscript. When an agent likes a query, they may ask to see a certain number of pages or chapters. If they don't specify, just send 50 pages.

Pitch letter – An agent's letter to an editor telling them why they absolutely need to buy a book the agent is shopping.

Pre-empt – When a publisher really likes a project, they may make an aggressive offer in order to pre-empt an auction (also known as "taking the book off the table"). The agent and author then have to decide whether to accept the offer or take their chances with an auction.

Print on demand (POD) – Copies of a book printed to order. POD is sometimes used as a blanket term for self-publishing, but POD may also be used by publishers to fill orders for backlist titles.

Print run – The number of copies a publisher prints of a book. There is an "announced" print run and an "actual" print run, and the difference between these numbers is something probably best not discussed.

Publisher (company) – The company that publishes your book.

Publisher (person) – A publishing executive who runs either a publishing division or an imprint and who typically has final say over what gets published.

Query letter – A letter describing your book, which will hopefully make an agent want to read more.

Reserves against returns – Since publishers usually calculate royalty statements within six months after publication, sometimes returns (see "Returns") will lag behind the statements. Since an author is paid based on net copies sold, this creates a conundrum because publishers don't really know what the net will be for quite some time after a book is published. In order to account for this, publishers hold a "reserve against returns" for the first couple of royalty statements after a book's publication, which means they hold back a certain amount of money in anticipation of returns. The reserve should be a reasonable amount (talk to your agent), and they should not hold a reserve forever (see also "Net copies" and "Royalty statements").

Remainder – Sometimes when a book isn't selling a publisher will sell off their remaining stock as a remainder, which means at a very low price. This is usually a sign the book is going "Out of print."

Retail price – The price of a book as listed on the cover. Often royalties are paid as a percentage of the retail price of a book.

Reprint – a) May refer to a publisher going back to press to print more copies. This is good. b) May refer to a publisher bringing out a new edition of a book that has been previously published.

Returns – Bookstores are almost always able to return unsold copies of books back to the publisher for a refund. This causes a great deal of chaos (see also "Reserves against returns").

Reversion – When your book is out of print, you may have the right to "revert" your book, depending on your contract language. Basically, this means the contract is canceled and the author can sell the rights to a new publisher.

Royalties – The amount an author receives on every net copy sold of their book (see "Net sales"). Royalties are either based on the cover price of a book or on the net amount received (see "Net amount received") by the publisher. An author does not receive royalty payments from a publisher until their advance has earned out (see "Earn out").

Royalty period – The accounting schedule for royalties. Most major publishers calculate royalties twice a year and send the agent/author statements and payments several months after the close of a royalty period.

Royalty statement – A statement of gross copies sold, net sales, subrights income, returns, reserves, money owed, advances paid, lunar cycles, cake recipes, and ancient Egyptian prophecies. Royalty statements may or may not be completely incomprehensible to anyone who has not spent years working in the publishing industry. Bonus points for illegibility.

Season – Publishers organize their titles by season. Typically, there are three seasons a year, which might mean that one publisher's "Spring" really means "Winter," while another publisher's "Spring" really means "Spring." Keeping publishers' seasons straight is a nearly impossible task, although for some reason everyone seems to know what "Fall" means. The Mayans they are not.

Second serial – Publication of an excerpt in a magazine or journal after book publication (see also "First serial").

Self-publishing – When an author arranges for their own publication and distribution. Sometimes (though less frequently now) referred to as "vanity publishing" and "POD," although self-publishing, vanity publishing, and POD have slightly different meanings and connotations. Vanity publishing usually refers to a service where the author pays to have their book published, self-publishing is more of a blanket term and may or may not involve paying up front, and POD has more to do with the process by which the book is produced (see "POD") than the self-publishing itself.

Sell-in – The amount of copies that are ordered by bookstores, libraries, etc. prior to publication. You want this to be a high number.

Sell through – See "Net sales."

Separate accounting – In a multi-book publishing deal, separate accounting means the books are accounted individually at the amounts specified in the contract. For instance, in a $100,000 book deal that is separately accounted, one book may count as $60,000 and one as $40,000 for the purpose of earning out. Since this tends to make it easier for an author to earn out sooner and one book might be a bigger hit than another, separate accounting is usually advantageous for the author. This is distinct from joint accounting, where the books under one contract are accounted together (see also "Earn out" and "Joint accounting").

Slush pile – Much maligned, much feared, and much sneered at, the slush pile is a repository of hopes and dreams for the authors who populate it and a Herculean and Sisyphean task for those charged with clearing the pile away to make way for the deluge still to come. The slush is full of half-baked ideas, the truly out-there, and the very occasional undiscovered gems, but it is mostly filled with good, solid efforts by perfectly respectable writers who are up against simple math that simply isn't in their favor. Ahem. Where was I? Oh, right. The slush pile is the submission queue for an agent or publisher. In the days of emails and databases, it is not usually a literal pile.

Subagent – An agent who sells subsidiary rights on behalf of a primary agent. Subagents are most common with translation and film/TV rights.

Subsidiary rights (Subrights) – These are all rights under the sun that aren't original print publication rights, such as excerpt, adaptation, film/tv, audio, translation, first serial, second serial, merchandising, etc., etc., and I mean it, etc. Some of these are retained by the publisher, who may exercise the rights themselves or sell them to third parties, and some of these rights are retained by the author. When they are sold by the publisher to third parties, the revenue is called "subrights income," which is subject to a certain percentage split between publisher and author as specified by the contract. Subrights income counts toward an author's revenues, thus helping an advance to earn out.

Synopsis – A summary of a work that covers the major plot points and characters.

Term of copyright – Most contracts for original publication in the US are for term of copyright, which literally means for the length of copyright, and the author only gets the rights back if the book goes out of print and the author reverts the rights (see "Out of print" and "Reversion").

Term of license – Sometimes contracts are for a set number of years. Terms of license are usually either based on the contract date or on the date of publication.

Tie-in – An edition of the book that ties in with a movie or TV show adaptation, usually featuring the movie cover or TV art.

Trade paperback – Mid-size paperback. Most self-published books are formatted in trade paperback size.

Territory – The countries in which rights are granted in a publishing contract.

Unearned – When an advance has not earned out, the book is said to be unearned.

Warranty – The part of a publishing contract where the author swears on their life that they are not plagiarizing anyone and everything is on the up and up (see also "Indemnity").

Wholesaler – Companies that get books to bookstores, libraries, etc. Unlike distributors, which fill orders for one or a few publishers, wholesalers fill orders for basically everything under the sun. Prominent wholesalers include Baker & Taylor and Ingram.

OBEY THE 10 COMMANDMENTS FOR THE HAPPY WRITER

Writers aren't generally known as the happiest lot. In case you think this is a new development, an 1842 letter from Edgar Allen Poe to his editor surfaced in which he was found apologizing for drinking so much and begging for money.

But believe it or not, writing and happiness can, in fact, go together. Here are ten ways for a writer to stay positive:

1. ENJOY THE PRESENT

Writers are dreamers, and dreamers tend to day-dream about the future and concoct wildly optimistic scenarios that involve bestsellerdom, riches, and interviews with Oprah Winfrey. In doing so, they forget to enjoy the present.

You know how it goes: "If only I could find an agent, then I'd be happy." When you get an agent, it then becomes: "If only I could get published, then I'd be happy." And so on.

The only way to stay sane in the writing business is to enjoy every step as you're actually experiencing it. Happiness is not around the bend. It's found in the present.

Because writing is pretty great; otherwise, why are you doing it?

2. MAINTAIN YOUR INTEGRITY

With frustration comes temptation. It's tempting to try and beat the system, whether that's by having someone else write your query, lying to the people you work with, or, you know, concocting the occasional fake memoir.

This may even work in the short term, but unless you are Satan incarnate (and I hope you're not), it will steadily chip away at your happiness and confidence, and your heart will shrivel and blacken into something that they show kids in health class to scare them away from smoking.

Don't do it.

3. RECOGNIZE THE FORCES THAT ARE OUTSIDE YOUR CONTROL

While it's tempting to think that it's your fault if your book doesn't sell, or that it's your agent's fault, or the industry's fault, or the fault of a public that just doesn't recognize your genius, a lot of the time it's just luck not going your way.

Chance is big in the book business. Huge. Gambling has nothing on the incredibly delicate and complex calculus that results in a book taking off.

Bow before the whims of fate because chance is more powerful than you and any agent combined.

4. DON'T NEGLECT YOUR FRIENDS AND FAMILY

No book is worth losing a friend, losing a spouse, or losing crucial time with your children. Hear me? No book is worth it. Not one. Not a bestseller, not a passion project, nothing.

Friends and family first. Then writing.

Writing is not an excuse to neglect your friends and family. Unless you don't like them very much.

5. DON'T QUIT YOUR DAY JOB

Quitting a job you need to pay the bills in order to write a novel is like selling your house and putting the proceeds into lottery tickets.

You don't have to quit your job in order to write. There is time in the day. You may have to sacrifice your relaxation time, your sleep time, or your reality television habit, but there is time. You just have to do it.

6. KEEP UP WITH THE PUBLISHING INDUSTRY NEWS

It may seem counterintuitive to follow the news of a business in which layoffs often constitute the bulk of the headlines, but it behooves you to keep yourself informed. You'll be happier (and more successful) if you know what you're doing. And agents and editors will appreciate your publishing savvy.

7. REACH OUT TO FELLOW WRITERS

No one knows how hard it is to write better than the people who have tried to do it themselves. Their company is golden.

Reach out and touch a writer. Plus, the Internet allows you to reach out to writers without smelling anyone's coffee breath.

8. PARK YOUR JEALOUSY AT THE DOOR

Writing can turn ordinary people into raving lunatics when they start to believe that another author's success is undeserved. Do not begrudge other writers their success.

Even if they suck.

9. BE THANKFUL FOR WHAT YOU HAVE

If you have time to write, you're doing pretty well. There are millions of starving people around the world, and they're not writing because they're starving. If you're writing, you're doing just fine. Appreciate it.

10. KEEP WRITING

Didn't find an agent? Keep writing.

Book didn't sell? Keep writing.

Book sold? Keep writing.

OMG an asteroid is going to crash into the planet and enshroud it in ten feet of ash? Keep writing. People will need something to read in the resulting permanent winter.

ACKNOWLEDGMENTS

This guide would not be possible without the people who have read my blog and contributed valuable comments over the years, so thank you to everyone who reads it and participates in the community.

Thanks so much to the fantastically talented professionals who helped me with this guide: Christine Pride for editing, Bryan Russell for copyediting, Dale Pease for designing the interior and cover, and Mari Sheibley for designing the cover of *How to Write a Novel* and creating the template for future guides.

Lastly, thanks so much to publishing industry professionals Jenny Bent, Tess Callero, Sarah LaPolla, Natasa Lekic, Laura Blake Peterson, Mike Shatzkin, Rachel Stout, and Mitchell Waters as well as author friends Lisa Brackmann, Christina Lauren, Tahereh Mafi, Sarah McCarry, Ransom Riggs, and Michael Schreiber for lending their expertise and support.

ABOUT THE AUTHOR

Nathan Bransford is the author of *How to Write a Novel* and the *Jacob Wonderbar* series (Dial Books for Young Readers). He was formerly a literary agent with Curtis Brown Ltd. and writes a popular blog about writing and navigating the publishing process at blog.nathanbransford.com. He lives in Brooklyn.

Made in the USA
Coppell, TX
23 January 2023

11556051R00144